LIFE SKILLS FOR TEEN GIRLS

BOOK 1 OF 3: UNDERSTANDING YOUR BODY & EMOTIONS

MARIA ANDERSON

MAZLOWE PUBLISHING

To download the Free accompanying Workbook:

Scan the QR code below or type the address in your browser:

https://tinyurl.com/TeenGirlsMA

📚 **GET the next books in the series**
✨**FOR FREE**✨:

Scan the QR code below or
type the address in your browser:

https://tinyurl.com/TeenGirlsMA

© Copyright – Mazlowe Publishing 2024 – All rights reserved.

The content contained within this book may not be reproduced, duplicated or transmitted without direct written permission from the author or the publisher.

Under no circumstances will any blame or legal responsibility be held against the publisher, or author, for any damages, reparation, or monetary loss due to the information contained within this book. Either directly or indirectly. You are responsible for your own choices, actions, and results.

Legal Notice:

This book is copyright protected. This book is only for personal use. You cannot amend, distribute, sell, use, quote or paraphrase any part, or the content within this book, without the consent of the author or publisher.

Disclaimer Notice:

Please note the information contained within this document is for educational and entertainment purposes only. All effort has been executed to present accurate, up to date, and reliable, complete information. No warranties of any kind are declared or implied. Readers acknowledge that the author is not engaging in the rendering of legal, financial, medical or professional advice. The content within this book has been derived from various sources. Please consult a licensed professional before attempting any techniques outlined in this book.

By reading this document, the reader agrees that under no circumstances is the author responsible for any losses, direct or indirect, which are incurred as a result of the use of the information contained within this document, including, but not limited to, — errors, omissions, or inaccuracies.

CONTENTS

A VERY BRIEF INTRODUCTION	1
A VERY BRIEF OVERVIEW	1
HOW TO USE THIS BOOK	2
A FEW GROUND RULES BEFORE WE MOVE FORWARD	2
FINAL THOUGHTS	4
CHAPTER 1	5
CHAPTER OVERVIEW	5
ACTIVITY TIME — A MOMENT TO BOND	5
GROWING PAINS	6
PUBERTY: IT'S NORMAL, DOESN'T MAKE IT EASY	7
(TYPICAL) PHYSICAL CHANGES	8
HEIGHT CHANGES	9
FEELING ANTSY?	9
WEIGHT GAIN	10
YOU AREN'T GETTING FAT	10
(TYPICAL) HORMONAL CHANGES	11
ACNE	11
ODORS	12
BODY HAIR	13
CAN I CONTROL MY HORMONES?	14
(TYPICAL) COGNITIVE DEVELOPMENT CHANGES	15
MENSTRUATION	17
PREPARING FOR MENARCHE (YOUR VERY FIRST PERIOD)	18
THE BIG LEAD UP TO THAT FIRST PERIOD	18
MENARCHE	19
THE MENSTRUAL CYCLE	20
BODY IMAGE AS YOUR BODY CHANGES	28
BEWARE THE ALMOND 'PARENT'	33
ACTIVITY TIME — HOW TO APPRECIATE YOUR BODY	35
ACTIONABLE WAYS TO CARE FOR YOURSELF	36
BASICS OF REAL SELF CARE	36
HOW TO SLEEP BETTER	37
HABIT BUILDING: DO THIS, NOT THAT	39
EXERCISE	39

EATING WELL	48
ACTIVITY TIME — THE BALANCING ACT	54
CHAPTER 2	62
CHAPTER OVERVIEW	62
EMOTIONAL CHANGES AND PUBERTY	63
UNDERSTANDING YOUR EMOTIONS	66
MANAGING YOUR EMOTIONS	72
ANXIETY: WHAT IS IT?	79
CAUSES, SIGNS, & WHAT ANXIETY MIGHT LOOK LIKE	80
WHEN ANXIETY STARTS TO TAKE OVER	82
MANAGING ANXIETY IN PRACTICE	85
NEGATIVE SELF-TALK: WHAT, WHY, & REFRAMING	86
HOW TO STOP NEGATIVE SELF-TALK	87
EMOTIONAL CONTROL IN ACTION: EMOTIONAL INTELLIGENCE	92
ACTIVITY TIME — GROUNDING TECHNIQUES	97
References	101

A VERY BRIEF INTRODUCTION

WELCOME

Let's cut to the chase: you purchased these books for a reason. It could be that you're a teenager, trying to figure out how to navigate the chaos of life. It could be that you're the parent of a teenager, looking for ways to guide them and even connect with them.

Whatever has compelled you to open these pages, welcome.

A VERY BRIEF OVERVIEW

In this book, we're going to discuss several topics. While the content might vary, here's what you can expect to find in each chapter:

- An overview of the specific topics to be discussed, including trigger warnings
- Hands-on exercises, some for parents and teens to work on together, some of them solo
- Real-life stories from real-life people who went through what you're going through
- 'For the teens' boxes. Their purpose? To make you check assumptions or frustrations

- 'For the parents' boxes. Same goes for you—to get you to see things from a new angle
- Recaps for teens and parents for easy reference at the end of each chapter
- **Bolded** words, which you can reference back to by using the appendices at the end
- A list of resources (also in the appendices) if you want to read about any topic further

HOW TO USE THIS BOOK

The purpose of this manual is for it to be practical, functional, and overall serve as a guideline for navigating the many life changes that happen to us from ages 13 to 18. I suggest working through the topics together—parent and teen, side-by-side—but there's no need to work through the topics linearly.

Each chapter the subjects within relate to each (because life doesn't exist in a vacuum!) but each is also standalone, with information, exercises, and takeaways related to that particular topic. This means that this book really is supposed to be useful: jump to whatever part you need to jump to, and then head to the appendices to check out additional resources as you need.

Pro-Tip: download the workbook / notebook we have created (refer to page 1), just for these exercises. That way you can refer back to your notes, musings, and ideas, all in one safe spot.

A FEW GROUND RULES BEFORE WE MOVE FORWARD

Like any good guide, I need to lay out a few rules before we jump into what might be difficult or triggering topics for some individuals. The point of these instructions isn't to order you to behave or think a certain way, but to set up good boundaries and make sure we're respectful.

RULE 1: KEEP AN OPEN MIND
As teens and parents alike work through these pages and especially the exercises, there may be some tough conversations. Remember that communication is key and try not to take offense.

RULE 2: TURN YOUR EARS ON
Remember to take turns talking. Parents, lecturing does no good. Teens, ignoring your parents just because they are speaking does no good. Turn your ears on. And while we're at it, make sure you're really listening to one another and not just forming your next thought.

RULE 3: THERE ARE NO DUMB QUESTIONS
No, for real. There is no such thing as a dumb question and no need to be embarrassed if you *do* have a question. Let curiosity take over and forget about judging or being judged for now.

RULE 4: SET YOUR BOUNDARIES
Teens, maybe you want what you're working on with your mom to stay private between the two of you. Moms (or dads, or guardians!), respect that request for privacy as long as there's no threat of self-harm. These are hard conversations to have and it's important to have trust.

> **FOR THE TEENS**
> I don't know if you gravitated toward this book yourself or if someone bought it for you, but here's the bottom line: you are going to grow up and experience intense, life-altering changes over the next few years. The shift from teen to adult can be both beautiful and stressful but ultimately it's pretty darn cool. So use this book, reference it, and know you're not alone.

> **FOR THE PARENTS**
> The beauty of teenage-dom is watching your kid mature into the little human you always dreamed of. The pain may be that you're not their go-to for the tough stuff or maybe you've drifted and need some help. That's what this book is for—work through these chapters together, because at the end of the day, it matters most that you keep showing up.

FINAL THOUGHTS

TEENS:

You've got this, let's learn and grow together. The best is yet to come.

PARENTS:

Ground yourselves and let go of that ego—just be there for your kid.

CHAPTER 1

Empowering YOU to Embrace Your Own Unique Body

CHAPTER OVERVIEW

IN THIS CHAPTER, we're going to work through several topics about the physical changes you might experience as a teen. We'll discuss some of the challenges you might go through as your body grows and develops, and we're going to talk about (and practice!) ways to appreciate who we are and embrace these changes. Finally, we're going to talk about how to be adaptable and practice ways to stay in tune with our physical selves.

> *"You have been criticizing yourself for years and it hasn't worked. Try approving of yourself and see what happens."* —Louise Hay

ACTIVITY TIME — A MOMENT TO BOND

Let's preface these tough and maybe uncomfortable conversations with a quick activity. Since you are hopefully working through this book together (teens and parents), it might be useful to spend a couple of minutes reconnecting so that you are both open to working together.

So let's spend a few minutes laying out our expectations for working together.

Teens: Be honest and tell your parents why you may be apprehensive about doing this book together. Are you worried they'll judge your questions or worries? Are some of these topics really embarrassing?

→ Give your parents an example of a time where they really supported you, and ask them to emulate that same behavior.

→ Give your parents an example of a time when you felt like you weren't being heard or seen, and offer a way to improve that as you work together through these topics.

Parents: Be honest with your teen—maybe share an anecdote about your own early teen years that might have been hard for you. It could be a funny example, or one where you felt like you weren't being heard by your own parents.

→ Ask your teen to communicate and be open to hearing their concerns, without panicking or judging!

→ Give your teen an example of a time when you thought you communicated well and ask them what worked about that communications style, so that you can work through these topics openly and effectively

Remember teens, you're not alone, even when it can feel like it—you just have to be willing to ask for help. And remember parents, that you, too, once went through these same struggles—and a little empathy goes a long way.

GROWING PAINS

I won't gaslight you: the physical changes that occur during your tween to teen years can be some of the most difficult and—let's face it—are sometimes the most painful ones. There's a reason we tend to refer to these changes as "growing pains."

I'm not just talking about your period (although we *will* talk about period pain in depth) but rather growth spurts throughout your entire body. When I was growing up, I remember shooting up four inches over one summer, every bone in my body achy and uncomfortable. I remember being freaked out when my breasts started to get larger and trying to hide this fact under bulky t-shirts. And I especially recall how I used to run into every single door frame or stair banister because I had no sense of my body and how to occupy space.

When we talk about physical change in teenage girls especially, it can be easy to be dismissive of the pain, discomfort, and very real connection between the physical and emotional. We're going to talk about emotional development in later chapters, so for now, let's talk about the physical challenges you might encounter or are already going through. In this chapter, we're going to start with puberty, talk in great depth about your period, followed by body image, and finally, discuss self-care. Let's jump right in!

PUBERTY: IT'S NORMAL, DOESN'T MAKE IT EASY

In its simplest form, puberty is a fancy word for how your body changes from childhood into young adulthood. It's rapid, it's unlike anything you've experienced (except when you were a baby), and honestly, it can be kind of awkward.

Sometimes, you will notice the obvious changes, like getting taller, but a lot of the changes happen inside your body, too. The physical changes that happen during puberty are crucial to you growing up. Unfortunately, you might feel a little bit like the odd person out as you go through puberty, because it happens at different rates for different people. Just remember that you are not alone!

> **FOR THE TEENS**
> Grab your notebook and go ahead and make a list of questions before you read this chapter. If at the end, you still have more questions or unanswered ones, write them down to talk about more with your parents, doctor, or other trusted adult. Remember, there is no such thing as a dumb question. A lot of this information might be new or weird, so ask for clarification!

> **FOR THE PARENTS**
> Maybe the hardest job when it comes to discussing puberty is to make your kid feel seen, cared for, and listened to. They can feel out of control, which can be frustrating and overwhelming for them. So, take a deep breath and be ready to guide them through it. And remember, this is not a one and done conversation: start these talks early and make sure you keep them going as your child continues to experience these changes.

(TYPICAL) PHYSICAL CHANGES

Puberty can look different on everyone, and honestly, this fact can be frustrating for you for many reasons. Maybe you wish you could slow it all down and stay a kid for a little bit longer. Or maybe you want to look like your friends and classmates who are already going through physical changes. Whatever you're feeling, just know that your reactions are totally normal, but unfortunately, there isn't a lot you can do to control when your body will change.

That being said, let's look at the typical timeline for when girls experience puberty.

Ages 10-11 years old:

- The first signs of puberty *usually* start around 10 years old.
- Growing breast buds is one of the first signs of puberty. Sometimes, each breast will grow at a different rate, so don't let that stress you—this is very normal!

- You might get kind of tall kind of fast. You might feel uncoordinated and clumsy.

Ages 12-14 years old

- Around age 12 is *usually* when the typical signs of puberty will become more apparent.
- You'll probably get your first period during this time, but don't freak out if it's not completely regular. It takes time for your body to adjust to these massive changes.
- You're also going to start growing lots of hair all over your body which is totally normal!

> **FOR THE PARENTS**
> Your kid might ask for a training bra, because breast development can be uncomfortable and let's face it, embarrassing for her. Remember, if she asks for one, respect her privacy and try to help normalize the fact that her body is and will continue to change.

What else can you expect to happen as your body continues through puberty? Read on to learn more about height, weight, and hormones.

HEIGHT CHANGES

We call it "growing UP" for a reason! We're not talking small height changes but really significant ones—some people might grow a lot at once and not grow again. Others can grow several inches in a few short months, followed by slow growth, followed by several more inches. As women, we typically reach our full height by the time we graduate high school.

FEELING ANTSY?

Usually, getting taller is no big deal. Clothes might suddenly be too short in the arms, legs, or waist, so go ahead and ask your parents to keep a few clothes in bigger sizes on hand so that you can wear what you feel comfortable in.

And sometimes, getting taller *can* be painful. Not necessarily painful as if you had an injury, but your body might feel sore or even just out of whack as your limbs stretch up or out. You might feel restless. Maybe you need more sleep or you might find sleep really difficult. My advice is to be honest with your parents about your discomfort, and parents, to take the pain seriously.

WEIGHT GAIN

Hear me and hear me well: bodies are supposed to gain weight. You are not supposed to weigh the same amount at 15 years old that you did at 10 or that you will at 35. Bodies change, we grow muscle, we have fat. There is no exact amount you are supposed to weigh, there are only healthy habits to build and maintain as you grow up.

> **FOR THE PARENTS**
> Throw away the scale. I mean it. Weight means nothing. Of course there are healthy ranges, and it's your job to keep your kid healthy. An active, muscular girl is going to weigh more and all the scale is telling her is that her value is tied to a number. Read that again: scales tie self-worth to numbers, and that is simply ridiculous. So toss the scale. And read on for ways to track your daughter's health that are actually useful and will benefit her in the long run.

YOU AREN'T GETTING FAT

You aren't fat, you *have* fat. And fat is no big deal—it's very much a natural part of our physical makeup and kind of critical to survival. Now, it is important to acknowledge that puberty will increase the amount of fat you have on your body, but this is expected and normal and absolutely not something you should try to avoid. Your body is starting to produce something called **estrogen**, which we'll get into in a little more detail below, but for now, know that this hormone is contributing to an increase in body fat.

Puberty is your body's time to grow up, so it's especially important to eat healthy and well. Why? Well, because your stomach is growing. Your bones are growing. Your organs are growing. Your body is demanding more food so you have even more energy to keep up this intense growth cycle over the course of the next few years.

Your job is to let your body grow. Make sure you're eating lots of good foods, packed full of nutrients. And don't overthink indulging in your favorite snacks. Remember: food equals energy! We're going to talk about how to build healthy eating habits later in this chapter.

(TYPICAL) HORMONAL CHANGES

Probably one of the more complicated and more subjective challenges with puberty are hormones. Hormone changes are a completely normal part of puberty, and it's these chemical changes in your body that are helping you grow up.

Remember just a few paragraphs up when I mentioned **estrogen**? Well, this particular group of hormones has a lot of influence on how puberty manifests in girls, ranging from breast development to changes in the reproductive system. Hormonal changes are critical to you growing up, but they can come with a few undesirable side effects. This does NOT, however, mean that you have to suffer.

Read on to learn more about some of the more common hormonal changes you will experience during puberty and ways to deal with them.

ACNE

Probably one of the most obvious signs of puberty and growing up: acne. Now, just because you are starting to go through puberty does NOT mean that you are guaranteed to have acne. Some girls can experience really light acne that can pop up when hormone levels change during their period. Others might have more aggressive bouts of acne, which can cover more of the face and even be painful at times.

There are different types of acne, including blackheads, whiteheads, and pimples. Different types of acne are linked to different chemical changes in your body.

WHAT CAN I DO ABOUT IT?

Unfortunately, you may not be able to control the severity of any acne you experience. But there are a few things you can try. Of course, always talk to your doctor if you are in pain!

- Start using a hydrating face-wash and fragrance-free lotions.
- Watch how sugar might be triggering your acne and limit it when you can.
- Drink a lot of water—it really can help your body feel better.
- Be careful not to overwash your face! Natural oils on your face are important and overwashing can actually make your acne worse and dry out your skin.
- Makeup is fun, but consider letting your skin breathe as much as possible. Avoid heavy foundations and wash your face every single night before you go to sleep.
- If you are having issues with pain, talk to your parents and arrange to visit a dermatologist—a special doctor who can help you figure out what to do for your skin.

ODORS

Hormones bring new and unexpected body odors. Odors might come from your armpits as well as from your genitals. This is because your body is creating new sweat glands—ones that bacteria like to cling to. These smells are nothing to be embarrassed about but it does mean you will need to rethink your approach to hygiene.

Consider finding a deodorant that works for you: could be natural or a more common brand, could smell like flowers or eucalyptus. When you shower, be sure to wash your armpits, inner thighs, and the area around your genitals thoroughly—but NEVER put any soap inside of your body; this can be harmful and lead to rashes and infections.

You might start sweating more than you did as a kid—or at least now you might notice more smells along with the sweat. Make sure you're washing your clothes regularly and wash your bras at least once a week for hygiene and odor purposes.

BODY HAIR

The social pressures around body hair are finally changing at long last, and I am here for it! Puberty is a time when you'll notice a significant increase in the amount of hair you grow on your body. You're going to find hair pretty much everywhere: from your legs and arms to your pubic area to your belly. Body hair is a natural and normal part of being human, and it is completely your decision how or even if you want to do anything about it.

Some girls like to shave their legs, others don't. In fact, a lot of athletes—male and female alike—shave their legs so as to be even more effective in their sport (think swimmers or cyclists!) Others still might wax or thread. And some people never remove a single hair.

The point is: don't feel pressured to shave, or try it, and feel free to never do it again. It is your choice!

If you *do* decide to shave, here are a few golden rules to follow so you practice good hygiene and stay safe around razors:

- Have an adult or older sibling show you how to shave and keep an eye on you for the first few times so you remember the steps and practice good habits.
- Don't shave dry skin, unless you're using a razor designed for that. Instead, opt for a cream or shaving gel so you don't cut your skin.
- Try to avoid cutting your skin, because this can lead to infections. But if you do knick yourself, it's not the end of the world—just rinse your skin and be careful of lotions. Apply

cold water and pressure to the wound and tell your parents if you are having trouble with the cut.
- Never share your razor: sharing can lead to infections and is not safe.

> **FOR THE PARENTS**
>
> To shave or not to shave? Try to let this one be your child's choice. It sounds like such a minor act in the grand scheme of life, but this is one of the initial pressures a young girl might face from her peers. Maybe she wants to try it, maybe not. Just remember (and remind her!) that she can always change her mind.

CAN I CONTROL MY HORMONES?

There is a long answer and a short answer, so I'm going to give you one right in the middle: you can control your hormones through medication—although this tends to be for more extreme situations, like your period is unbearably painful or you have a medical condition. This is a conversation to have with your parents and your doctor, if you feel like you need more help.

That being said, you can try to *regulate* your hormones, which will help you feel like you're maintaining some control while also giving you a chance to learn about what your specific body needs. This isn't a comprehensive list, but just a few ideas of ways you can adjust to make these intense changes a little more manageable:

- Catch some zzz's. Seriously—we joke about teens needing sleep, but there are a lot of studies that support the importance of sleeping and even napping. So hit snooze.
- Move your body! Exercise produces endorphins, a natural chemical that can boost your mood and help you feel more content. Try out a new activity if your old ones aren't enough or if you just need a change of pace.
- Up your fat intake. Might sound weird, but eating healthy fats helps our bodies grow and our brains work by helping us

process other foods. The key takeaway is that fats help us balance our sugar levels which helps our hormones. Go ahead, indulge in guacamole.
- Watch out for over-processed foods: sometimes, when we talk about healthy eating, we use words like 'avoid carbs and sugar' when really, we're talking about avoiding refined carbohydrates. Carbohydrates are crucial to a healthy diet, so think about limiting PopTarts, not pasta or potatoes.
- If you're having acne woes, consider trying out different face washes until you find one that works. A lot of different brands have travel-size bottles so you don't have to buy full bottles. Just be careful to avoid so-called acne scrubs—a lot of these (unless dermatologist recommended) can do more harm than good. That's because the rough bits in the scrub can cut your skin as they exfoliate, creating micro-abrasions that can get infected and cause worse skin problems..

The other catch to managing your hormones? A lot of patience.

I know this might be totally frustrating advice to hear, but now is the time to give yourself a little bit of a break. You are going through a lot of change. Maybe you've had the chance to talk about puberty in depth before now, or maybe you haven't. Regardless of how much you do or don't know, talking about these changes is going to be a lot different than experiencing them.

(TYPICAL) COGNITIVE DEVELOPMENT CHANGES

Now, we're going to talk much more about your emotional development in the next part of this book, but let's briefly touch on emotional and cognitive changes you might be going through during puberty.

We often notice cognitive leaps more readily in babies and toddlers—having no concept of danger to suddenly being scared of objects that they used to not notice. There are similar cognitive developments that happen during puberty and while sometimes daunting for everyone involved, it's a good sign that your brain is maturing.

Teens, you might notice changes such as:

- Feeling more emotional. No, not behaving dramatically (although life can feel that much more intense!) but rather your anger might be angrier, your sadness, sadder.
- You start to feel stronger about who you are, or spend more time trying to figure out who you are. You desire independence and control.
- You may feel more self-conscious and start to be annoyed by how you think others are perceiving you.
- You might start thinking about people sexually, like a crush that's way more intense. This is completely normal but can be confusing.

Parents, society often presents the tween/teen years as horrifying, but let's change this narrative. That's not to say there aren't tough moments—there are. But let's look at both sides of this picture so you can help your kids and stay sane.

For example, you might notice:

- Your teen being grumpy toward you—but remember, just like when they were babies, you are their safe person. They are experiencing complicated emotions, and they have to be able to work through them and will try them out on the person they trust most.
- All your teen wants to do is sleep, but this is probably because their body, mind, and emotional intelligence are all changing at an insanely rapid rate! Sleep is crucial.
- Your boundaries are being tested. As a parent, you have to enforce the rules but you also have to make sure that the rules continue to make sense. The concepts of independence and sense-of-self really start to manifest during puberty, so try not

to take your child's rebellion personally. Evaluate where you can give some freedoms while keeping her safe.

We're going to talk about emotional intelligence a lot more in Chapter 2, but just know that these big, emotional changes start in puberty and continue as your kid grows up.

Speaking of big changes... Let's jump into one of the most profound physical developments you'll go through during these early teen years: menstruation.

MENSTRUATION

I've gone ahead and created a separate section about menstruation, aka your period, because this is a robust topic that deserves some special attention. We're going to explore the different phases of menstruation and take some time to talk about normal changes when it comes to your period. We're also going to talk about how to advocate for yourself when it comes to your physical, emotional, and social needs when you are having your period.

Remember that menstruation is a normal part of puberty and nothing to be ashamed of, embarrassed by, or feel icky about. People the world over get periods, this is part of life.

STORYTIME

Remember earlier, in the intro, when I told you that I'll be sprinkling in stories from real women all over the world? Here's one for you, in case you ever feel embarrassed about your first period or don't quite know what's going on—it happens to everyone!

> "When I was younger, I liked to eat in my bed—like full meals, not just snacks. Well, one night, I took my food to my bed and ended up falling asleep with the plate, fork, and knife next to me under the blanket. The next morning, I woke up to blood on my sheets. I was totally convinced I had hurt myself in the middle of the night and had no idea what was going on! Turns out, I got my first period. But I stopped eating in bed after that…"

PREPARING FOR MENARCHE (YOUR VERY FIRST PERIOD)

The very first period you experience can be really weird, so let's hold space for your feelings: there is nothing wrong with being nervous, having questions, or being unsure about the whole situation. I know that I was scared to get mine, because I didn't really understand or talk to anyone about it before it happened.

Even though getting your period is a big step toward growing up, remember that knowledge is power. And I promise you that if you educate yourself and ask all the questions, your period will be a lot less daunting and maybe you can help your friends, too.

> **FOR THE PARENTS**
> Menstruation is a normal part of growing up, although nothing about it feels normal. Give your daughter space to complain, feel uncomfortable, snuggle on the couch and do nothing. At the same time, remember to validate her pain and pay attention to how bad it might be—there are real medical issues to look out for, so watch for the signs.

THE BIG LEAD UP TO THAT FIRST PERIOD

Remember how earlier we discussed the physical changes in your body, like your breasts developing and growing hair everywhere? Well, these are the very first signs that you are going to start your period sometime within the next few years of puberty.

Another clue that your first period is coming in the next few months to year? You are going to start experiencing a thin discharge (like thin mucus!) from your vagina. This is one hundred percent completely normal—although admittedly weird at first. This white-ish fluid is just your body preparing internally as new (good) bacteria prepare your body for your menstrual cycle.

Fun fact—this vaginal discharge is not only totally normal, it is super important to keeping you clean and free from infections! Remember when I said NEVER use soap inside of your body? That's because this liquid you're going to start noticing is your vagina's way of self-cleaning. It's acidic, too, so you might notice that after a while, your underwear might look like they have bleach spots.

Now, once you start having a regular menstrual cycle (which we'll talk about soon), you'll see different types of fluid at different points throughout your cycle.

Just remember, talk to your parents or another trusted adult if you have any worries or questions!

MENARCHE

Your very first period is called '**menarche**.' In the medical field, this is just a fancy word used to describe that you are at peak puberty and will now have a menstrual cycle.

Unfortunately, you cannot predict when or where you'll get your first period, but there are a few clues so you can make an educated guess:

- Typically, you'll probably get your first period anywhere from 11-16 years old. The timing depends on when you've gone through the first signs of puberty and even genetic factors. The average in the United States, for example, is 12 years old.
- A few days before you get your first period, you might have a bad stomach ache, where it can feel like the insides of your lower belly are tight or squeezing together.
- Another big clue is that your breasts might be sore, as well as your lower back.

- Some girls might feel like their belly is bloated and gassy—like you ate something greasy.
- Another sign is that a few pimples might pop up on your face, since your hormones are adjusting to this next big step.

What can you expect from this first period? Well, it will probably last 2 to 5 days, and you might not get it again for several more weeks. This is because your body is still adjusting and growing, so "regular" cycles might take 2 to 3 years to develop. We'll talk more about a typical menstrual cycle next.

THE MENSTRUAL CYCLE

You may have heard this phrase a lot: **menstrual cycle**. But what does this even mean?

Your menstrual cycle relates directly to your reproductive organs—specifically your uterus and ovaries. These organs develop as you grow up, and the menstrual cycle is your body's way of preparing you to have kids of your own one day, if you choose to do so.

Specifically, the menstrual cycle is when your body sheds the lining of the uterus, signaling to your body that your eggs (and you have thousands of them inside of you!) won't become a baby and it's time to restart the whole process over again.

We call this process a 'cycle' because there tends to be a steady, cyclical timeline wherein these different phases take place. Every time you start your period, the cycle restarts. It might surprise you to learn that a menstrual cycle is in fact four different phases throughout a set amount of time (typically 4 to 5 weeks long) and not just your period.

When you're first getting your period, you may have anywhere from 28 days to 45 or sometimes more days between cycles—this variation is totally normal. Your body is still adjusting and growing and your menstrual cycle goes through the same process.

Around 2 or 3 years after your very first period, your cycle should be more regular—although that can look different for each person. If you have any concerns, speak up!

Here is a graphic that shows the 4 different stages of the menstrual cycle:

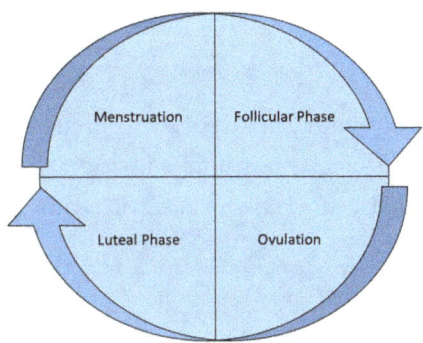

Menstruation

- Most commonly referred to as your period, menstruation starts your cycle
- Menstruation is when the uterus sheds its lining, 'dropping' an unfertilized egg
- A period is made up of a mixture of blood, mucus, and even cells
- A period typically 3 to 7 days, with heavier bleeding at the start and less toward the end

Follicular Phase

- This is the second phase of your cycle and lasts around 2 weeks
- There's a gland in your brain (the pituitary) that tells your body to make follicles (a little sac). One of these will eventually become an egg

Ovulation

- This phase is when the egg drops from your ovary and works its way toward your uterus by way of the fallopian tubes
- Ovulation happens one time a month, but can last for a few days

Luteal Phase

- The final stage of your cycle, the Luteal Phase is when your uterus (thanks to special hormones inside your body) decides if the egg that just came its way is fertilized or if you'll get your period.

> **FOR THE PARENTS**
> We aren't going to talk about sex in this book but now is a good time to talk to your daughters (and sons!) about safe sex. Sometimes we want to avoid these hard topics, but it's important to arm your kids with as much knowledge as possible so they make informed choices! Remember, kids have access to all kinds of information on the internet, so don't assume they are clueless – **they likely *already* know A LOT more than you think.** Your role is to vet what's real and normal. And your role is to make sure they can always come to you if they have an issue or concern, without being judged, no matter how weird, gross or explicit the subject is.

TRACKING YOUR MENSTRUAL CYCLE

We've talked about what your menstrual cycle is and the four different phases, so now let's talk about why and how to track it.

You need to know the ins and outs of your menstrual cycle for many reasons, including that you need to learn what normal and healthy looks like for you! It's always a great way to take charge of your health and be able to advocate for when something seems strange or concerning to you.

Here are some tips for tracking your cycle:

- Using a journal or the calendar on your phone, note the first day of your period (remember, this is the first day that you see blood)
- Although it won't be regular for some time, try to keep track of how many days your period lasts each month—but don't freak out if it changes each month for a while!
- It'll take a while to know how often you need to change your period products, but paying attention to how many pads or tampons you use on each day of your period will definitely help you feel more confident about what you might need to keep with you

SPEAKING OF PERIOD PRODUCTS...

We are really lucky to live in the 21st century because the products we have access to while we're on our period (and even throughout our menstrual cycles) have come a long way! Did you know that some women used to use moss as pads? Others opted for washable cotton scraps.

While these ideas were certainly innovative, modern period products are a little more hygienic and also allow you to figure out what works for your specific needs.

So what period products might you have access to now?

- **Pads**: Probably the most commonly used period product, pads stick to the crotch of your underwear on one side and rest against your body on the other. Pads can have different lengths (for overnight vs daytime), absorbency, and sticky wings to help them stay attached to your underwear. Pads are a great starting place if you're not sure what you want to use. They are also ideal for overnight use. There are also reusable pads.
- **Tampons**: Tampons are very common as well but can be trickier to understand how to use at first. Basically, a tampon made of super absorbent material (natural cotton among other things) that you insert inside of the vagina—don't worry, it

will not get lost inside of your body, that is impossible! Also, there's a little string attached to the end so you can pull the tampon out easily when it's time to switch it out. Tampons are nice because you really don't feel or notice them as much as pads. But you must be absolutely careful to change them regularly to avoid **toxic shock syndrome** (TSS).

- **Menstrual Cups:** This period product is gaining popularity over the last few years. Like tampons, menstrual cups are also inserted into the vagina but are incredibly eco-friendly and supposed to be reused. They're usually made of silicone and shaped like a funnel—it might take some practice to figure out how to use this product. It's also important to sanitize menstrual cups between periods.
- **Period Underwear:** Probably one of the coolest inventions out there, period underwear are exactly what they sound like: special underwear designed to absorb your menstrual blood and are completely washable and reusable. One perk of this product is that you're not harming the environment with disposable items *and* you don't have to stress about leaks— or you can double up for those heavy days without fear. There are all kinds of shapes and styles to choose from, so be sure to check these out.
- **Menstrual Disc:** One of the more rare period products, a menstrual disc operates similar to a menstrual cup in that it collects the blood, but unlike the cup, this disc sits in front of your cervix (a cup sits in the vaginal canal) and can be worn for much longer amounts of time. They tend to be very effective but a little messier and harder to use.
- **Free Bleeding:** Always an option, free bleeding is when you choose not to use any period product and instead let your body do what it does naturally. This choice can be daunting, but know that there are people all over the world who free bleed. A lot of athletes who are competing in day-long events free-bleed instead of having to worry about changing their pads or tampons.

In addition to the items that help collect the blood from your period, you might find it helpful to have some items on hand when you're menstruating (check out the list below!) Cramps can be uncomfortable, and often painful. Ever watched those period simulation videos online? Cramps are no joke.

Unfortunately, in addition to cramps, you might have a few other symptoms associated with your period and this will vary person to person. These can include back aches, headaches, low iron, food cravings, and period poops.

Yes, period poops are a real thing. We need to talk about this annoying symptom because yes, girls poop (insert eye roll here). So what is a period poop? Basically, as you prepare to shed the lining in the uterus (aka, your period), your body produces fatty acids (prostaglandins) to help the muscles relax. Well, these acids make *all* of your muscles relax, including the ones that control your poop. No, you won't poop your pants, but you may need to go more often.

OTHER ITEMS TO KEEP ON HAND DURING YOUR PERIOD

- Medications such as ibuprofen or another over the counter option are good to have in stock—just always consult your parents before you take anything. These meds can ease the cramps that come with your period, as well as alleviate other symptoms, like back aches or even mild headaches.
- Hot pads are another super useful item to keep around. You can buy an electric one, although options like clay or water might be more useful on the go. You can also make one yourself with a large sock and a pack of dry rice.
- Chocolate... this one is a little weird, but there's some science behind craving chocolate: it could be that your body needs an extra energy boost, and dark chocolate especially is loaded with antioxidants and magnesium.

FOR THE TEENS

Never EVER let someone dismiss your period pain. Periods can definitely be uncomfortable—remember what we said about cramps?—but you'll eventually learn what to do to take care of yourself. But you should NEVER be in severe pain. Under adult supervision, you can try over the counter meds like ibuprofen. But if you don't feel relief then you need to talk to a doctor and make sure that your needs are being addressed.

FOR THE PARENTS

If your daughter is in pain but her doctor dismisses her concerns, find a new doctor. We have finally reached a generation where women's health is a priority, and there is a ton of new research about menstruation and what can be done to help. Your daughter has a voice now—listen to her and be her biggest advocate!

HOW CAN I PREPARE FOR MY PERIOD?

The previous paragraphs are a good start to learn a little about the science of periods and what a **'menstrual cycle'** might look like.

I know the question you're asking: how do I avoid being embarrassed or caught off guard by my first period? While we can keep an eye out for symptoms, no, you can't predict the day you'll start your first period.

But you *can* be prepared by taking some of the following steps:

- Carry a couple of pads or tampons (or choice of product!) in your bag or keep some in your locker at school.
- Have a backup pair of pants and underwear at school or carry some in your backpack.
- If you need help, know which grownups you can talk to in different situations. For example, maybe your teacher or the school nurse, your parents, etc.
- If you get your first period and you're not with your parents, have a plan! Maybe you want to leave school early or maybe you need a change of clothes. Parents, make sure you discuss how your kid wants to deal with this experience and be ready.

- Practice putting pads in your underwear. You may opt for a different period product, but pads are definitely the easiest to use if you're on your own and need to handle your first period without help. But go ahead and practice, so you're comfortable when the day comes.
- Parents: if you have sons, give them some pads to hang on to for the women in their lives! And talk to them just as much about periods as you would your daughters—it's important to help normalize the conversations around periods.

A FINAL NOTE ABOUT PERIODS

It should go without saying, but I'm going to say it: having a period does not make you weak, less than, or 'emotional.' A period is a biological change to the female body that influences the reproductive system.

Now, periods can be weird and frustrating and that's okay—you have to get used to this new part of your life. At the same time, periods should never keep you from playing sports, climbing trees, riding bikes, running, playing, anything that brings you happiness.

WHAT CAN PARENTS DO TO HELP?

It can be tempting to behave in extremes when it comes to preparing your daughter for her period. Some parents refuse to talk about it more than once, worried they'll overwhelm their child. Others might go into waaaaay to many details, scaring their kid with things that might not end up applying to their situation.

I suggest the middle road: start the conversations about menstruation earlier, maybe around 8 years old. You don't need to go into every graphic detail just yet, but use the information above as a guide for conversations.

The other tip is to talk about menstruation regularly and normalize the conversation—this will help set the stage for your kid to come talk to you whenever they have questions.

Let's say your daughter (who may be reading this book alongside you) is older and much closer to getting her period or may have even started menstruating. It is still important to continue to talk openly about menstruation, how it can change as she ages, and guide her through any questions that may come up, including safe sex talks and candor about birth control.

The other piece of this puzzle? Normalize talking about periods for the boys and men in the family, too. Brothers should be told all about menstruation, so they know how to support their sister and appreciate what she is going through. In fact, consider having them carry a pad or two in their bags, especially if they go to the same school as their sister. Dads, go buy your daughter pads and chocolate, and let her know that you can offer a different kind of support.

The bottom line is to have frequent, open conversations about menstruation.

BODY IMAGE AS YOUR BODY CHANGES

We talked earlier about how your body is going to change thanks to puberty, but we haven't spent a lot of time talking about how you might be *feeling* about these changes.

> So let's take a minute here and now:
> How are you feeling?

It's okay if the answer is scared. It's okay if you're feeling totally chill about everything so far. It's even okay if you're kind of angry. What's important is that you're completely honest with how you're feeling because your thoughts, worries, and opinions matter.

How do these points tie into **body image**? Well, you have one body and how you view yourself—how you talk to your body—is connected to how you feel about your body. And while your feelings are going to change and adapt as you grow up, it's important to listen to your voice first, before taking on the opinions of the wider world.

WHAT IS BODY IMAGE?

Hold up a mirror: this is body image.

I'm only (kind of) kidding. The concept of **body image** is really about how you see yourself, (literally) and sort of how you see others seeing you—in other words, you might start to feel peer pressure because of the physical changes your body is undergoing thanks to puberty.

For example, you may be suddenly more attuned to how tall you are or how much you weigh. Maybe you're focusing on your hair color, how your skin looks, or even how clothes fit you.

Body image is also about perception—which we're going to talk about further in just a few paragraphs. But the basic idea is that, as your body changes, you might be viewing it in a way that isn't exactly real, or that maybe is being influenced by someone or something else.

WHY TALK ABOUT BODY IMAGE?

As you go through puberty and as your body starts to adapt to these new, physical changes, you will likely become more self-aware of how you look, maybe even comparing yourself to your friends or classmates. Becoming more aware of your body is a very normal part of growing up—but it can be confusing to know how to react to these changes and how to handle other peoples' comments about you.

What you think of your changing body might be affected by both internal and external ideas: maybe you have older sisters or cousins, and wonder if your body might look like theirs. Or you could have a skewed view thanks to social media. As for internal factors, you might be worried that your breasts are taking 'too long' to develop or that you're actually pretty okay with having hair on your legs.

A MOMENT FOR REFLECTING…

Before we jump into more information about body image and how it might be affecting you, take a moment to answer the questions below. Remember, try to be honest with yourself:

- Are you being critical of your body in any way?
- What do you really love about your body, now that you're growing up?
- What frustrates you about your body?
- Do you have good role models to talk to about your body questions?
- Are you listening to YOUR voice before you listen to your peers' opinion?
- Are others being respectful toward your body as it changes?
- Are you being respectful toward others as they go through their own changes?

I'm posing these questions not as a one-time prompt, but as questions that you should come back to, whenever you feel like you may be getting caught up in the noise of how bodies should or should not look.

PERCEPTION: BODY IMAGE IS MORE THAN PHYSICAL

When we talk about changes to your body, we're not just talking about noting the physical differences. We are also talking about your emotional state—like the power of your words inwardly and toward others. Our emotions have a huge impact on our perception of the world, and also how we let others influence (or not influence!) our feelings.

Let's talk about this idea more…

It's a pretty typical part of puberty to hyper-fixate on your body's changes. You are getting taller, maybe rounder or perhaps leaner. What if your hair has changed color or maybe you started wearing glasses?

These attributes are just physical changes—not much we can do about them!

But what happens when we apply an emotional lens— *perception*—to the physical changes?

Perception (how we understand our body, or even view other people's bodies) can be positive, negative, or even neutral. The experts who study this idea break down body image into a few different categories:

- What you think you see: For example, you might view your body as too fat just because you've gained a few pounds. Maybe you think your breasts are too small, because your classmate wears a bigger bra. What you actually look like is not what you see.
- Seeing affects your feelings about your body, which unfortunately can make you spiral toward bad habits, like dieting or trying to change your physical appearance through harmful means.
- Seeing and feeling influences how you think about your body, and can lead to you thinking about your body from specific mindsets, rather than as a physical thing.
- And the three ideas above? These lead to behavior changes, which are stepping stones into a whole world of toxic culture around beauty standards, diet fads, and harmful habits.

Let's be real for a minute: you are absolutely allowed to wonder about your body and have doubts about how you're physically changing. I'm telling you this because, even if you do your best not to bow to social or environmental pressures, something may still get to you at some point.

What matters is how you respond to it, and stay true to yourself, your needs, and how you want to perceive your body.

Speaking of…

OTHER PEOPLE'S OPINIONS REALLY DON'T MATTER

For centuries, women and girls have been pressured to look a certain way. These pressures tend to come from society, where collective beliefs have influenced clothing, hairstyles, body-shape, and even demeanor.

Fortunately, women and girls of the 21st century are finally tossing these absurd ideas in the trash and, as a whole, we are all striving to be less influenced to be or look a certain way, but instead listen to ourselves and our bodies.

Here's an example: when I was growing up, there was a wild misconception that what you weighed was more important than your physical composition. Unfortunately, this meant that a girl who was muscular, athletic, and strong, and who happened to weigh something outside her healthy range, would be told to lose weight—her physical value suddenly tied to a number. Now, this young girl, who's body image prior to this advice might have been pretty positive, is suddenly obsessed with losing weight to meet a number on a scale rather than listen to her body. She can no longer perceive her body accurately.

We now talk about weight a little differently, citing genetics, height, build, muscle mass, and even different stages of puberty as having a role in that scale number. Unfortunately, the damage is still done, and it'll take a few more generations before we completely change this negative narrative.

Which brings me to this point…

Should you even care?

It's easy to tell you to brush off other people's opinions. But it's harder to do so in practice. You'll be bombarded with advice and thoughts and opinions nonstop—and you can't always tune it out. It's a real flaw of social media (which we're going to talk about in depth in a later book) but also of our social settings.

And, sometimes, even our family can negatively influence how we view ourselves. Maybe you notice it when you're being compared to a sibling, or maybe someone is making comments about you needing a bigger size of clothing or that your body hair is showing. These comments aren't always intended to be critical, but they can really mess with our heads if we're not confident in our bodies and in our minds.

BEWARE THE ALMOND 'PARENT'

I'm not a huge fan of people tagging the word 'mom' onto this trend, because dads can have just as much positive or negative influence on their daughters' body image. In any case, this is a topic that deserves discussion.

An 'almond parent' can exhibit one or both of the following behaviors:

- Overly criticize their child's physical appearance and comment on their eating habits. For example, refusing to let their daughter have a snack hours before dinner, or insisting that she eat just an apple but not the peanut butter because it's fattening (FYI: peanut butter is good for you!)
- The other type of almond parent doesn't necessarily comment on their child's body, but rather leads by (poor) example. Maybe they eat half a salad and claim to be full, or refer to having a few french fries as 'cheating.'

Parents, both of these points are more for you than the teens, because, as we learned when our kids were babies, they are always watching us, listening to how we speak to ourselves, observing our cues for how they should then treat themselves.

But teens, it may be helpful to be open with your parents if they *are* nitpicking your eating habits. There will be an exercise at the end of this chapter to practice having conversations about building positive habits around eating and exercise.

STORYTIME

> "I really wish someone had explained to me just how much
> OTHER PEOPLE'S OPINIONS DON'T MATTER.
> I used to be scared that if I didn't listen to my friends about how I should feel about myself, I wouldn't have friends or people would think I was weird. I think this was especially hard for me during middle school, because we were all going through a lot of change and none of us really knew how to talk about it.
> But now that I'm older, I've realized it's way more important to be true to who you are, and you will eventually find people who like you, just as you are! They might not be your classmates and you might feel lonely for a while, but I promise, your people are out there."

Still struggling to cope with your new shape amid building social pressures? It's okay, I promise! But here are some expert tips for getting your mind in a more positive space when it comes to thinking about your body:

- Focus on your strength: my legs are so strong!
- Wear clothes that feel good to you—and feel free to change it up and try out new styles.
- Remember: clothing size DOES NOT MATTER. Seriously, find a pair of pants in the 'same size' from two different brands and compare how different they are.
- Dance, move, roll, wiggle: let your body be a body.
- Avoid social media: these images are NOT REAL.

> **FOR THE PARENTS**
> Here's a tip for combating negative body image—or rather, to help your daughter avoid over-focusing on her physical appearance at all: compliment anything but her looks. Did she absolutely crush it in a sport? Admire her prowess. Did she ace a test? Applaud her brain. How about her sense of humor? Tell her how funny she is. Our bodies are just a tiny part of who we are—so help her focus on her whole self.

ACTIVITY TIME — HOW TO APPRECIATE YOUR BODY

You may or may not keep a journal, so just know that this short activity is going to mimic journaling: using the guidance below, let's spend a few minutes being appreciative.

When it comes to puberty and all of the changes you're experiencing, you might be finding it difficult to feel grateful or excited about your body. While it's completely understandable that you may be experiencing mixed emotions, it can be easy to let your internal criticisms spiral out of control. So let's counter this negative habit with a positive one!

First, grab some sticky notes (or, if you prefer, you can write on the blank sticky notes below).

Now, write down three things (one per sticky note) that you appreciate about your body right this minute. Try to be as specific as possible. And try to show appreciation for something that you might normally feel insecure about. Take that negative thought and flip it on its head by complimenting yourself!

Some examples:

→ I am proud of how strong my legs are—I can run, jump, dance, and move with such powerful limbs!

→ My curly hair is so lush and thick— I can do so many cool hairstyles with it!

→ I really like wearing glasses because the frames are like another fun accessory to show off my style!

Now, after you've written your three appreciative thoughts, take those sticky notes (if you've written them here, transfer them to real sticky notes or a piece of paper) and stick them somewhere prominent. I recommend your bedroom mirror.

Each and every day, read these appreciative thoughts aloud to yourself. And believe in them.

ACTIONABLE WAYS TO CARE FOR YOURSELF

We've talked about puberty, we've talked about menstruation, and we've talked about how to keep an open mind about your new body (and how you might view it).

So how about we discuss some tangible ways to help your body as you grow up? For the next few paragraphs, we're going to dive into some basics of self-care—but not the fluffy kind where I suggest you paint your nails. No, I mean hands-on ways to keep yourself strong, healthy, and living your best life as you learn to care for yourself in new ways.

BASICS OF REAL SELF CARE

We're going to cover three topics in this section: Sleep, Eating Well, and Exercise. There are definitely other ways to practice self-care (who am I kidding, I really love getting my nails done!) but these are the basics, the starting points. Once you have these concepts down, then you can start thinking about self-care habits more specific to YOU.

SLEEPING

The importance of sleep cannot be over-exaggerated. There's an old saying that goes 'when you sleep, you grow.' There's definitely an element of truth to this idea.

Your body needs rest. Think about it this way: if you've ever run a race or played a sport or danced a recital, you are physically tired afterward. The same goes for your brain—as we talked about before, puberty is when your emotional and cognitive functions are having their own mega growth spurt. These changes are like running mental marathons on repeat.

Combine the physical changes your body is experiencing with the cognitive leaps your brain is now making: it's time to take a nap.

Parents, let your teen rest.

Teens, read on to learn how to get better sleep and what risky behaviors to avoid when you don't have time to sleep and what to do instead.

HOW TO SLEEP BETTER

EXERCISE

We're going to talk about the importance of exercise in the next section below, but it's top of the list for helping your body rest better, especially at night. Exercise can look different depending on your physical ability, but the main idea here is that you need to keep your body active during waking hours. Exercise will help settle your restlessness (thanks, changing body) and relax your mind (you'll be too tired to think!). We'll talk about specific exercise tips in the next section.

EAT WELL

You are what you eat. It's kind of gross to think about food that way, but let's break it down.

- **SUGAR**: We need sugar—sugar is critical to our bodily function. But sugar asks as a booster, aka it gives you a boost of energy before you come crashing down. Sometimes, we crave sugar when our body is overly tired. And while eating

might help keep you going, it's good to opt for a nutritious snack instead of a candy bar. You can get that same boost of energy without the crash afterward.
- **HYDRATION**: Drinking the right amount of water each day can help you sleep better because water is the single most important liquid to put into your body. Try to drink between x amount and x amount of water each day. You'll find two things start to happen. First, the better you hydrate your body, the more you'll crave that same amount of water each day. Second, you'll feel less foggy and more able to focus. Both of these will help keep your body regulated and feeling good.
- **FUEL UP**: You cannot go to bed hungry. Please, read that again! Food is crucial to survival and going to sleep with a content belly is key to a good night's rest. We'll talk about the pressures of diet culture in the section below, but here's how food relates to sleep: a full stomach (but not stuffed) means that your body feels like it will have enough energy in it to allow you the ability to relax and rest.

WIND DOWN TIME

Screen time is not a new phenomenon and one that scientists are studying much more in depth with new generations. While cell phones and computers play an important role in our society today, technology is impacting our sleep, and not for the better. Some studies show that you should stop using electronics at least an hour before bed—this means no phone, TV, computer, or eReader. Other studies have found that you should try to avoid electronics for several hours before sleep.

We're going to talk about the pros and cons of technology in our chapter on social media and safety, but for now, know that the little computer in your pocket is messing with your sleep.

HABIT BUILDING: DO THIS, NOT THAT

You should build your sleep habits based on your particular needs, but it can be hard to know where to start with figuring out what works for you. Use the table below for some straightforward tips that you can adapt for your own specific situation.

TRY THIS	NOT THAT
If you're hungry, have a snack before bed	Avoid snacking after dinner just 'because'
Take a warm shower in the evening	Skip showers, especially after exercising
Read a book, color, or listen to music	Doom scroll social media for hours on end
Restless? Try to learn some cool dance moves you've seen, do some stretching	Toss and turn nonstop in bed
Consider an earlier OR later bedtime	Stay up just to stay up
Wake up earlier so you have calm time	Sleep in until you're rushing and stressed

EXERCISE

We talked about exercise in the context of sleep, so let's talk about the benefits of exercise on its own! In this section, we'll do a quick review of the physical and mental benefits of working out, discuss the specific benefits during puberty, and look at different types of exercise and how to find something you'll enjoy doing so you build good, life-long habits.

PHYSICAL BENEFITS OF EXERCISE

- Helps you build strong muscles and bones

- Improves your cardiovascular health (how your body pumps blood and oxygen!)
- Is great for all that restlessness that comes with growth spurts
- Will help you maintain a healthy body composition
- Consistent exercise as a teen will have long-term benefits fighting off potential ailments, like heart disease, diabetes, high blood pressure, and osteoporosis (bone weakness!)

EMOTIONAL BENEFITS OF EXERCISE

- Can help you find it easier to focus more on sedentary tasks (like schoolwork)
- Exercise produces endorphins, which helps your brain stay happy and positive
- May be part of a social outlet, helping you find new friendships
- Having trouble grasping your homework? Take a brisk, 10-minute walk and come back to it—even short bursts of exercise can reset our brains and clear our minds

Here's a helpful hint when it comes to exercise and consistency: you have to find a workout or activity that you LOVE. You may prefer group motivation or perhaps you like to workout solo. It's also important to try new activities, because your physical abilities are always changing!

The other crucial detail here is that you have to listen to your body! Rest days are just as important as super active days—our bodies need time to rebuild and heal so that we get stronger, faster, and more agile.

Now, let's look at the four 'types' of exercises and then jump into more specific ideas to help you get motivated to get your body moving!

TYPES OF EXERCISES

Experts typically divide exercise up into three different areas based on the physical benefits each type has on the body: aerobic, muscle-building, and bone-strengthening. I'm adding stretching/flexibility to this list, because flexibility plays its own important role when it comes to moving your body.

AEROBIC

Probably the most common type of exercise (because we do it daily!), aerobic exercise is when you get your heart pumping. There are three levels of aerobic exercise: light, moderate, and vigorous. Just like the names suggest, each level of aerobic intensity has to do with how much energy your body uses to complete that exercise. Health experts tell us to have at least 60 minutes of aerobic exercise at least 3 days a week—we'll talk about specific activities a little further into this section.

- **LIGHT AEROBICS**: Typically, light aerobics tend to be part of our daily activities. For example, you do light aerobics when you're walking around the house, doing chores, or even standing for longer periods. Walking up and down the stairs is another good example, because this could be a normal daily movement for you: your heart rate doesn't tend to get too elevated during these activities but you're not dormant, either.
- **MODERATE AEROBICS**: When you're exercising moderately, you might breathe a little bit harder, or start to sweat as you are moving around. This is how we define moderate aerobics. Typical activities could be dancing around to a great song, taking a brisk walk, or even helping your parents with yard work (like raking), which can expend more energy than, say, making your bed.
- **VIGOROUS AEROBICS**: As the name implies, this kind of aerobic exercise uses a lot of energy! Vigorous aerobic exercises are usually more deliberate—maybe you're playing soccer, or perhaps you've gone for a run. The idea is that you're intentionally pushing your body and heart to complete an activity.

MUSCLE-BUILDING

We get the point by now that puberty is changing your body's physical shape, right? Well, your muscles are part of your growth, and it's important to include muscle-building exercises into your daily routine.

There's a weird idea going around that exercises that build muscles (also called strength training) will make girls and women look 'bulky.' There's pretty much no basis to this rumor, and in fact, having strong, defined muscles often means that you might look leaner in appearance. And looks aside, having strength is super important to having a healthy body! Muscles support your joints, which means that you can participate in a huge range of sports and activities.

It's important to note that when it comes to building up your strength, you may have to start slower than you would say, being able to run a mile. That's because as we age, our muscles adapt along with us. And when you try out a new sport—like Jiu Jitsu, a martial art—you are going to discover all kinds of muscles that you may not have realized that you had before.

We'll talk about strength training (building your muscles!) when we look at examples of different types of exercises.

BONE-STRENGTHENING

Pretty similar to muscle building, bone strengthening is all about improving your overall physicality and increasing your bone density. You should aim to do bone-strengthening workouts at least 3 days a week, for about 60 minutes. These exercises can be part of your muscle-building workouts, as long as you are including bone-specific activities (which we'll get to!)

Bone-strengthening exercises tend to be all about impact and resistance, which also help with your muscles. These types of exercises include higher-impact workouts and definitely require effort. Some examples are jumping rope, jumping up and down on the ground, climbing, and even playing on a playground.

STRETCHING/FLEXIBILITY

As I mentioned earlier in this section, stretching and flexibility building exercises don't typically fall within the 'types of exercises' list. But building your body's range of motion (flexibility) and making sure you know what steps to help heal after hard workouts (stretching) are crucial to have a good relationship with exercise.

- **FLEXIBILITY**: It's all well and good to be super strong and be able to lift heavy objects. But what if you can't bend over properly to pick up that heavy object? Or what if you slip when roller skating—can you recover your balance quickly? This is where flexibility comes in. Being able to bend your muscles and limbs is pretty important when it comes to your physical performance. In fact, some sports require that you be so limber, you can do wacky things with your body, like dance under your own leg or fold your whole body like a pretzel. Ultimately, flexibility just means training your body to have a range of motion so that you can participate in any activity you want!
- **STRETCHING**: Some health experts argue that stretching is more important than actual exercise. I'm not sure I'd go that far, but stretching after a workout is key for two reasons. First, stretching helps untense your muscles so you don't experience spasms or tightness. It's normal to feel a little sore after a workout, but stretching can help reduce the discomfort. Second, stretching is really important for athletes because it can help reduce lactic acid buildup. Lactic acid is that super sore, completely unable to move, feeling you might get if you push your body too far, like having to play an extra few minutes in a game or hiking further than you were prepared for. A good, thorough stretch can increase your recovery time by days, so that you can get back to your active lifestyle quicker.

LET'S GET A MOVE ON!

We've talked about exercise and the science behind IT, so let's give you some real tools so that you can get your body moving and discover just how much you can do!

I like to plan my physical activities around my mood, how my body is feeling, and how social I feel like I want to be that day. To that end, below are several dozen different exercises and activities, broken up into three categories: ones you can do solo, ones you might do with a friend, and team / more social sports.

SOLO IDEAS: CLEAR YOUR MIND WORKOUTS

- Biking: indoor or outdoor. Just make sure you tell an adult where you are going
- Running: same points as above. Try trails, paths, pavement, or treadmill
- Dancing: crank up that music and move. Or see about private lessons
- Walking: the single best activity for overall health, a brisk walk makes everything better

BUDDY WORKOUTS: PUSH EACH OTHER FURTHER

- Tennis: great aerobic activity and fun to bond over this sport
- Swimming: make a game of it by swimming laps or chasing one another
- Hiking: reach new heights together, it's always safest to hike with a friend
- Solo activities can also be friend activities, so consider bring along a friend

GROUP ACTIVITIES: BOND OVER MOVEMENT

- Team sports: soccer, hockey, basketball, lacrosse, rowing, dance team, you name it!
- Cheerleading: a fantastic workout, team-building sport, and fun to boot

- Martial Arts: gain strength while learning how to take care of yourself and friends
- Surfing, skateboarding, rock climbing are all great for social bonding AND exercising

OTHER WORKOUT IDEAS

Pretty much all of the ideas listed above are some mixture of aerobic and strength-training (don't forget to stretch!). But did you know that there are exercises you can do that are designed to help build specific muscle groups? There are tons of videos online that can show you proper techniques. Or ask your parents for help, or even see if you can meet up with a personal trainer at your local gym.

And I hope this goes without saying, but I'll say it anyway: you can do anything you put your mind to! There's no rule that you can't do an exercise because some weirdo says it's only for boys. Try out anything and everything and continue with the activities you love!

- Build your arm strength through push-ups, pull-ups, dips, and presses
- Try out free weights (with help at first!) to do bi-cep curls, tricep curls
- Squats, lunges, fire-hydrants, and deadlifts will give you powerful legs
- For full body exertion, try mountain climbers, planks, and jump squats

> **FOR THE PARENTS**
> Helping your daughter have a positive relationship with her physical body means that you have to encourage her. As girls get older, society can tend to put them in boxes where they can have to behave more delicately or avoid getting messy or dirty. Your daughter can always take a shower. So encourage her to run, jump, climb, slam, fall. She has no limits.

A BRIEF DISCUSSION ABOUT LIMITATIONS

It's all well and good to talk about the benefits of physical exercise and offer you some ideas for what to do, but let's add a dash of reality to the conversation.

Depending on where you live, you may not have access to great outdoor areas. Maybe your school doesn't have funding for the sport you really want to play. Or maybe you have some physical challenges and need help adapting. Quite candidly, money can also be a factor when it comes to participating in more niche exercises. Maybe it's not safe for you to workout alone.

All of these reality checks aren't meant to discourage you, but rather let you know that you're not alone if you're feeling a little limited, and to offer some alternative ways of thinking so that you can get in the exercise you want and need so you can feel your best.

SAFETY

Some activities you should never do alone. For example, when hiking, it's easy to get lost or turned around on a trail. Always go with a friend, and always tell someone who won't be going with you where you plan to be hiking.

Another element to safety has to do with where you might be working out or playing. Make sure that an adult knows where you'll be and that you can call for help if you need it. We'll talk about this in a later book, but NEVER share your live location on social media or geo-tag your location if you do end up sharing a picture of you working out.

MONEY MATTERS

It's rough when something you want to do costs money and your family might not be able to afford it. But that doesn't have to be the end of the conversation!

If it's a sport, see if there is financial aid (from the school or club) to help pay for uniforms and away games. If it's classes, like ballet or karate, see if the instructor is willing to work with your parents on a different payment schedule.

And don't forget about amazing online resources! You can do all kinds of cool workouts and training for free thanks to YouTube and other exercise apps.

ADAPTING A SPORT

We all have our physical abilities and we have our own physical challenges. Sometimes, we live with these challenges, and sometimes we have an injury and so we have to adapt so we can continue being active.

Maybe you have a physical condition that makes it difficult for you to participate in certain activities as much as you would like. Fortunately, we live in a time where coaches and trainers can actually make quite a few adaptations, allowing for all kinds of bodies to be a part of the team.

Talk to your parents about the kind of exercise or sport you'd like to do, and go from there. Lots of schools and clubs have different levels of team (varsity, junior varsity, or club sports) and some even have adaptive equipment for different types of teammates.

YOU ARE LIMITLESS

You can do anything. You can build your strength. You can try out a new sport. You can fall down, because you can get back up. Push your body and then push it further.

And now that we've talked about pushing your body, let's talk about FUELING your body, by having a thorough look at building good eating habits to last you a lifetime.

EATING WELL

Do you suddenly feel like you're starving all the time? Do you have weird food cravings? We've already talked about how your body might crave different kinds of foods as your hormones change, but did you realize that you should start eating more, now that you've hit puberty?

In these next several paragraphs, we're going to dive into the topic of eating well, and specifically, how to build good eating habits.

FIRST, A COMMENT

Unfortunately, as a tween or teen girl, you're going to get bombarded with truly ridiculous advice about what to eat, what not to eat, that your pant size matters, that you shouldn't eat past a certain time of night, that snacking is bad, that certain foods are bad, that certain foods are good, that…

Okay, if you're dizzy from reading that paragraph, imagine what it's like to hear these things in real life. Except that, unfortunately, you probably don't have to imagine. You may have already started witnessing the dangers of diet culture thanks to social media, friends, even your relatives. Remember almond parents?

Diet culture is pervasive, but you don't have to succumb to it.

My goal in this section is to show you a simpler way of thinking, while also providing you with simple, straightforward guidance on healthy eating.

FOOD IS FUEL

Remember how much we talked about exercise and staying active? Well, you can't do that if you don't eat properly. Ever tried to work out hungry? Feels pretty darn difficult, huh?

Let's go back to an even more basic concept: you've hit puberty and now your body is growing. This means that your stomach, intestines, muscles, brain, heart—they are all growing, too! It's your responsibility to eat well so that your body has enough energy to fuel your growth. Not to mention that what you eat will affect your hormones, acne, energy, menstruation, and sleep.

We're going to talk about this idea of 'eating well' before we go any further.

EATING WELL

When I use this term, I'm not trying to prescribe any specific way of eating. You can be a vegetarian, eat meat, love pasta and hate rice, prefer salty over sugary.

The idea of eating well is really about understanding thorough nutrition, what your body needs, and making sure that you are in control of your eating habits.

Now, you might hear the word 'control' and automatically jump to the idea that I'm saying that you need to control how much you eat. But instead, I want you to learn about healthy habits so you can adjust to fit your reality. Love Oreos? Eat Oreos! Just not at breakfast, lunch, and dinner. Despise spinach? You're not alone. Try chard, kale, or another vegetable entirely.

The bottom line is that your teenage years are when you grow and develop, physically and mentally, and your eating habits have to reflect this fact. Let's jump into details about your changing nutritional needs.

VITAMINS & MINERALS

Remember before when I said that all those organs and bones are growing more rapidly now that you've hit puberty? Well, with increased growth, you not only need *more* food but you need different kinds of food to help your body function. We call these vitamins and minerals.

There are all kinds of different vitamins and minerals that we get pretty easily through eating, so let's focus on the three big ones that play the biggest role in helping your body grow and stay strong.

IRON

You can find the mineral, iron, in all kinds of food—from meat to beans to leafy greens. You absorb iron the best when you eat it with something that contains a lot of Vitamin C (like orange juice). Iron is super important because it helps move oxygen around your body. Sometimes menstruation can lead to lower iron levels.

CALCIUM

You're definitely too young for the 'Got Milk' commercials, but the point of those advertisements was to promote the importance of calcium. Just how much calcium you need increases dramatically as you hit puberty because, you guessed it, your body is growing. Calcium levels have a direct impact on the health of your teeth, bones, and muscles. And like iron, you can get calcium through all kinds of foods: cheese, milk, soya, yogurts, and tofu to name a few.

VITAMIN D

Just like when you were a baby, Vitamin D plays a super crucial role when it comes to building healthy bones. An added benefit of this super vitamin? It's a natural mood booster! You can definitely get Vitamin D through foods, like fortified milk. But you can also absorb it through sunlight. So if you're feeling a little low, go play outside and soak up the sun.

FIBER

Getting enough fiber is important to keep your internal system flowing. Fiber is really useful when you're having trouble going to the bathroom, and it can be a game-changer when it comes to feeling full and satisfied. Fiber rich foods include beans, oatmeal, and celery.

CARBS ARE NOT THE ENEMY

I wish I could go back in time and stop the dummy who started the trend that says that carbohydrates are bad for you...

Since I can't, let's clarify this point: carbs are just food. Food is made up of three basic groups: carbohydrates, proteins, and fats.

- **CARBOHYDRATES**: give us energy, keep our insulin balanced, and are basically pretty much every food we eat. A necessary staple for a healthy, strong body!
- **PROTEINS**: gives us a different kind of energy and helps support muscle growth. A good standard for protein consumption is to eat about 1 gram of protein for each pound that you weigh, every day, to keep building your strength. And when you're working out a lot, you need to increase your protein so your muscles can grow.
- **FATS**: a normal part of a lot of food, there are some fats that are healthier than others, but this isn't an all or nothing situation. Healthier fats include olives, nuts, dark chocolate, avocados, fatty fish, whereas we want to limit something called saturated fats. This doesn't mean you can't have saturated fat, just make sure you're not over-indulging. So go ahead, butter up your bread!

WHAT DOES A DAY OF GOOD EATING LOOK LIKE?

We've talked about how we categorize food, so what does this look like in practice?

This question is completely subjective, but I'm going to offer a few ideas to get you thinking holistically about food. Ultimately, YOU have to figure out what works for you.

BREAKFAST, LUNCH, DINNER, and EVERYTHING IN BETWEEN

- **BREAKFAST**: Set yourself up for success with a well-rounded breakfast. Consider eggs, toast, a bowl of fruit, and Greek yogurt. Or opt for pancakes, sausage, and some orange juice. Just fuel your body so that you have energy to get the day going.
- **MID-MORNING SNACK**: I'm a big fan of nuts, cheese, and fruit mid-morning, sometimes along with a protein smoothie

that is packed with fruit, too. It all depends on how hungry I feel and what activities I have coming up.
- **LUNCH**: This meal looks different all over the world, but the catch here is eating so you keep having energy but not stuff yourself so that you need a nap! Opt for a sandwich, apples and peanut butter, and a bag of chips. Or go a more fun route and bring something fun your family might have leftover, like a vegetable lasagna or BBQ chicken sandwich with coleslaw.
- **AFTERNOON SNACK**: Most people need a pretty big energy boost post-lunch and pre-evening. The afternoon snack is key to having enough energy to move on with the day. Try crackers with peanut butter or cheese, carrots and hummus, or guacamole and chips. A little sugar might help, but don't overdo it, since too much can lead to a worse slump than you were having.
- **DINNER**: Dinner looks wildly different, so I won't give specific ideas. But remember a couple of things about dinner. First, if you just got back from sports, you have to replace those calories so eat up! Second, you don't have to eat every single thing on your plate, but make sure to eat until you feel content (PARENTS, please note—the clean plate club is not cool and can harm your kid's relationship with food).
- **AFTER DINNER SNACK**: Movie night? Enjoy some popcorn. Cram session? I was a big fan of pretzels with peanut butter to help my mind stay active. There's no rule written anywhere that says you can't eat after dinner. Just listen to your body's cues, and if you're hungry, eat.

FOR THE PARENTS

Helping your daughter have a positive relationship with her physical body means that you have to encourage her. As girls get older, society can tend to put them in boxes where they can have to behave more delicately or avoid getting messy or dirty. Your daughter can always take a shower. So encourage her to run, jump, climb, slam, fall. She has no limits.

> **FOR THE PARENTS**
> It can be tempting to micro-manage our kids' eating habits. You should absolutely pay attention to how and what they eat but try to give your daughter some control over her food. If she really hates peas, why are you forcing her to eat peas? If she's still hungry, don't make a comment about the amount but instead ask what else she wants to eat.

LET'S TALK ABOUT INTUITIVE EATING

This term may be new to you, or you may have heard it before. Just like any eating advice, there's no single right answer for what and how you should eat. But what I like about the basics of this concept is that it encourages you to listen to your body before anything or anyone else. Intuitive eating is all about creating a balance between healthy habits and at the same time, partaking in less healthy foods because they are delicious or make you happy.

If there's one truth about restrictive food habits (aka diets), it's that they are not good for you. If you deny yourself your favorite food you're doing two things. Let's use a medium-sized chocolate chip cookie as an example (or just insert less healthy food craving here):

→ First: you will spend all your energy obsessing over how much you want that cookie.

→ Then: when you finally 'give in' and eat it, you might eat five instead of one, because your brain thinks it has to hoard.

Intuitive eating tries to break this way of thinking by saying, go ahead, eat that one cookie or even two, and overall, just make sure that most of your other meals are a bit healthier.

And if you want another cookie later, or maybe some fries? Cool, just keep it all balanced. Listen to your cues.

Unfortunately, society tends to bombard us with diet fads, social pressures, and prepackaged food, so you don't really have to think about how or what you're eating. This means that you need to train your brain and body to embrace what feels natural to you. Really wanting those chocolate chip cookies is neither good nor bad—it's your body saying, yum that sounds good and I need a sugar boost.

We're going to do an exercise next, but the idea of intuitive eating is a perfect segue into our next chapter, where we're going to look at trusting your inner self, and how intuition becomes an important part of your forming identity.

ACTIVITY TIME — THE BALANCING ACT

Let's wrap up this chapter with a hands-on activity about finding your balance. The idea of the 'right' balance is going to depend on each person. Maybe you're someone who finds joy by getting outside on solo walks. Or maybe you prefer spending quality time with family and friends.

The first step in this activity will look at how your current time, energy (physical and emotional), and needs are balanced. We'll spend some time plotting out where you are, here and now, is step one.

The second part of the activity will focus on what you want to change about your current balance, including how to practice goal setting.

BUT FIRST: WHAT DO WE MEAN BY BALANCE?

Life is all about balance. You have to go to school *and* you want to have fun. You want to buy concert tickets but you have to save up some money first.

But the idea of balance isn't just about opposites. Rather, it's about finding harmony between the things that you're obligated to do and the things you want to do. If you have to write a tedious paper, can you do so in a place that is comfy and keeps you calm? If you have to go to the doctor, is there someone or something you want with you so you feel safe?

These ideas will make more sense once you complete the exercise, so let's jump in!

BALANCING ACT — STEP ONE: PLOT WHERE YOU ARE AT RIGHT NOW

You can use the chart below to 'plot' where you are at in your life right now, based on the topics. Try to be as honest about your current state —mental, physical, emotional— because this will not only help you understand where you might be struggling (or succeeding!) but also help you set goals as you continue to grow up.

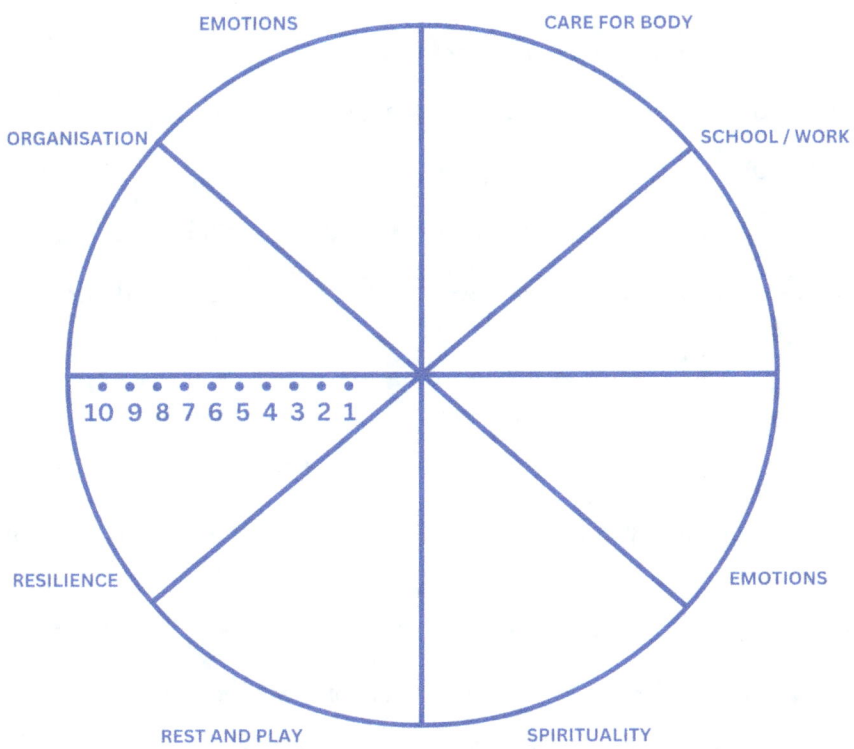

ORGANIZATION

→ How well are you managing your life right now?

→ Are you feeling frenetic or are you generally in control of your time?

EMOTIONS

→ Are you happy with how you handle yourself when you experience different emotions?

→ How do you feel about your current communication skills?

CARE FOR BODY

→ How do you feel about your current habits related to food, hygiene, and exercise?

→ Are you kind to and about your body?

→ Do you treat yourself with respect and patience?

SCHOOL

→ Do you feel like you are thriving in your academic life?

→ Are you satisfied with your level of effort to be a good student?

RELATIONSHIPS

→ Do you feel like you can confide in and trust your family?

→ Do you feel like you can rely on your friends?

→ Are your family and friend relationships able to handle the tough stuff?

SENSE OF SELF / SPIRITUALITY

→ Do you feel like you know who you are and who you want to be?

→ Do you practice habits that bring you joy, peace, and promote your sense of self?

REST / PLAY

→ Are you getting enough sleep *and* downtime?

→ Do you enjoy the activities you participate in?

RESILIENCE

→ Are you able to adapt to change or pivot when something goes wrong?

→ Does the idea of the unexpected overwhelm or excite you?

→ Do you find that you are often stressed or are you able to handle your daily life?

PLOTTING YOUR CURRENT STATE

Using the questions above as guidelines, plot your points on the chart.

Plotting a "10" means that you are completely satisfied with your current status in this area. To plot a 10, place your dot on the respective line and toward the outer edge of the circle.

Plotting a "1" means that you feel dissatisfied or unhappy with your current status in an area. To plot a 1, place your dot on the respective line and toward the inner edge of the circle.

Remember, there are no right or wrong answers! The point of this exercise is to give you a visual of where you feel like you are at currently.

PLOTTING YOUR DESIRED STATE

So now that you've seen where you're at... where do you want to be?!

Using the same plot and graph style, we're going to practice goal-setting using the chart below. If you want your "Care for Body" goal to be a 7 instead of a 2, you're going to write down a goal that helps get you there.

I've laid out some examples of achievable goals by topics, but they are just ideas. YOU set your goals. It's okay to make them super small and super simple— just start somewhere.

AS YOU THINK ABOUT YOUR GOALS

The goals you set for this exercise should be action-oriented and achievable. Try to give yourself a reasonable timeline to set and meet each goal. And be sure to stick to them— if you can't or it feels daunting, adjust until you find a way to really put these goals into action. And as you reach your goals, you can always come back to this activity and set new ones!

ORGANIZATION

→ Every Sunday, I will repack my school backpack for the week so I can make sure I have all of my usual supplies.

EMOTIONS

→ For one month, I will spend five minutes each day practicing deep breathing to help regulate my emotions. And during this month, whenever I'm triggered, I'll try to remember this practice.

CARE FOR BODY

→ For one week, I'll try out taking a night shower instead of a morning one, so that I can spend whatever amount of time I need without feeling rushed to be done.

SCHOOL

→ I will visit the after-school tutor for history class once a week for one month and see if this helps me understand this topic more.

RELATIONSHIPS

→ For the next few days, I'm going to put my phone down whenever I'm in person talking with my friends, so I am more present and they feel like I'm actually listening to them.

SENSE OF SELF / SPIRITUALITY

→ I'm going to journal for five minutes every night for the next week, and I'll write about what I really liked about myself today and where I wished I'd done something different.

REST / PLAY

→ For the next week, I'm going to turn off all electronics at least one hour before I go to sleep. Instead, I'll read, play a game with my family, or work on some art.

RESILIENCE

→ For the next week, whenever I'm feeling stressed about school, I'm going to express my worry to my parents instead of letting it get out of hand.

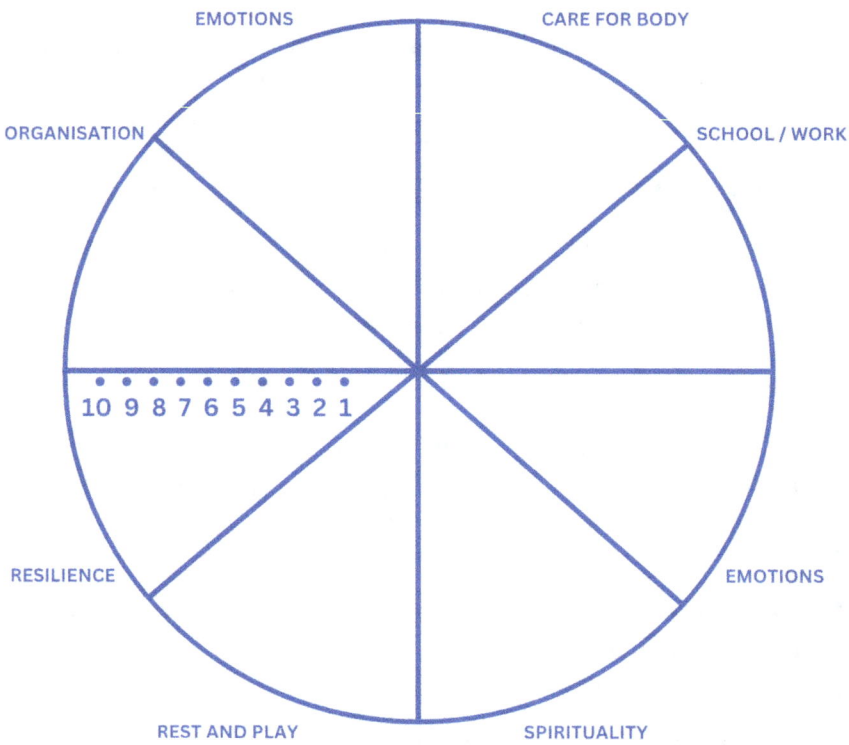

Remember, you can always revisit this exercise! Use this tool to evaluate your life whenever you start to feel out of balance or if you need to set some new goals to help keep you in balance.

The next chapter will offer additional tools for helping you understand and manage your emotions.

CHAPTER 2

Understanding Emotions:
A Guide to Navigating Your Inner World

CHAPTER OVERVIEW

IN THIS CHAPTER, we're going to talk about emotions. We'll look at the emotional changes that happen thanks to puberty, and then we'll talk a little bit about why it's important to manage your emotions. After that, we'll take a look at how to interpret or understand emotions, including negative self-talk and anxiety, both of which can start to take over during puberty. Finally, we're going to discuss ways to develop your emotional intelligence, which is a fancy way of saying being aware of and keeping control over your emotional state. As usual, we're going to wrap up the chapter with an exercise, this one focused on 'grounding techniques.' Let's jump in!

"I don't want to be at the mercy of my emotions, I want to use them, to enjoy them, and to dominate them." —Oscar Wilde, The Picture of Dorian Gray

EMOTIONAL CHANGES AND PUBERTY

We've spent a lot of time talking about how puberty is more or less responsible for your fluctuating emotional state these days. Now, we're going to look at some of the details behind what is going on in that mind of yours—and why your emotions might feel like they are all over the place these days. We're also going to talk about the range of emotions you might be experiencing. Because trust me: you're not the only one going through these changes!

UNDERSTANDING YOUR EMOTIONS IN PUBERTY

Let's start with a breakdown of some of the internal and external variables that might be affecting your emotions.

HORMONES

We won't dive into this topic much more, but one point should be repeated: hormones play a huge role in your cognitive, physical, and social development. You can't really control hormones, but you can learn to work with them.

For example, a lot of girls and women get irritable a few days before their period (commonly referred to as PMS). No one should ever tease you about your period, because your body is going through a real hormonal change that you have no control over—it's all the chemicals inside your body that are causing such an array of emotions.

That being said, you can try to put yourself in your preferred social situations if you know your hormones might dominate the day. I'm not just talking about when you're about to get your period, but any ol' day when you feel like your emotions are taking over. For example? Make Friday night plans to have a chill movie night in with your best friend instead of surrounding yourself with classmates who might make you upset or edgy.

SLEEP

We talked a lot about sleep in the previous chapter, but what I'll touch on here is that sleep—lack of OR over-sleeping—can have a huge impact on your emotions. The amount of sleep you need on any given day might vary but it's good to try to stick to a schedule that meets your needs. Parents, building good sleep habits might take a little compromising: maybe bedtime can be pushed a little later, as long as there's no more screen time with it.

PHYSICAL CHANGES

Probably one of your most immediate stressors (something you might be stewing over) are the physical changes your body is going through. You may be a bit obsessed with how you look, or how you think other people might be judging your growth and development. I can't tell you to stop worrying because that doesn't do any good. But what I can say is that you and your classmates are all going through the exact same changes (at varying paces). Yes, even that girl who looks like she's got her life completely together is stressed about all of the puberty-related questions. You're not alone, even if your peers aren't as willing to talk about it.

SCHOOL STRESSORS

Maybe you love school, but that doesn't stop it from being pretty darn stressful from time to time. Tests, moving on to more advanced classes, more homework, less free time: all of these things are happening at the same time that your brain and body are developing, and I really wish you didn't have to do it all at once. Over-achieving (or feeling like you have to do it all) is a real risk at this age—doesn't mean you can't give school your all, but make sure to pencil in some down time.

On the flip-side, you might start to under-achieve, thanks to the pressure. Maybe you're feeling overwhelmed and instead of doubling down on school, you stop trying completely. Sometimes, the stress gets so bad (or maybe you get a bad grade) and you suddenly feel like you can't do it. What's the point of trying, it's not important...

We're going to talk about negative self-talk—and how to reframe your thinking— later in this chapter, so if you're feeling a little disheartened, don't worry, we'll talk about it.

OVER-SCHEDULED

Speaking of down-time… parents, is your daughter involved in way too many activities? Does she have an after-school job? Does she study all weekend long? How about her extracurriculars? For some reason, we tend to think busy kids are happy kids. Or, if we're being honest, we think over-scheduling their lives will keep them out of trouble.

But more often than not, teens who want to experience life will do so, schedule or not. Try talking to your teen honestly about how they spend their time. Together, figure out how they can build in a little more free time to do things just for the fun of it, not the grade or the trophy or the money. (Parents, it's okay to let your teen relax).

ANXIETY

What is anxiety? It can be a mental state of mind, or it can be a more chronic (prolonged) condition. Anxiety during puberty can look similar to stress but the biggest difference is that stress is more often related to a singular event or problem. Anxiety is more constant and consistent—some people describe it as being caught in a spiral or loop of stress, fear, and worry. We're going to talk a lot more about anxiety in one of the sections below.

FEELING A LOT OF EMOTIONS?

I'll go ahead be candid: you have the right to be 'emotional.' You can have bad days, you can have mad days. Your mind, body, brain—basically every single thing about you—is in change mode and that's not always easy. You can also have happy days, joyful days. And you can have days that are just sort of days, filled with moments where you're happy or mad or sad.

Now, just because you're experiencing some wild changes doesn't give you permission to be deliberately unkind, cruel, hurtful, or rude. I know it can be tempting to just snap—trust me, I have had my moments of being meaner than I meant to.

You can apologize, but sometimes, the damage is done. So wouldn't it be better to instead try to avoid hurting others' feelings (and your own!) by managing your emotions?

That's what we're going to touch on in this section: benefits of understanding your emotions and how to take that understanding and turn it into managing your emotions. Why do we need to talk about managing how we feel? Well, I can say 'be nice' or I can show you *how* to be nice. That's what a tool does: it gives you options for how to respond to a situation.

UNDERSTANDING YOUR EMOTIONS

Having emotions or feeling certain ways about life, experiences, or people is not new for you—you've had emotions your entire life.

WHAT'S CHANGED?

Well, for starters, your hormones, which we've talked about at length in the previous chapter. Not to mention that your brain is undergoing some serious cognitive change—you're making leaps and bounds when it comes to understanding the world around you, and that can set off some pretty intense emotions. A big part of why you might be feeling so conflicted about life is that you are developing your sense of self, and along with that, your perspective of the world.

Emotions play a vital role helping you develop these perspectives because it's sort of your brain's way of teaching you how to read situations and people.

Emotions are often reactionary. So let's work through an example together: A classmate insults you, calling your choice of clothing outdated or frumpy.

Let's say you respond with aggression: The information you internalize is that people who insult your clothes make you mad—so you respond to everyone with those same general behaviors with aggression. To the point where someone might point out that you're missing a button and you get angry at them for pointing out a flaw, which isn't exactly fair.

Or maybe you cry. Or maybe you laugh it off because your sense self says that that person's opinion doesn't matter.

The risk with emotions is that they aren't always reliable. Aka: they are based on your perception of a situation or an encounter, and not necessarily what's actually going on. It's a little bit like a blind reaction, because you don't always know what you're about to see or the other person's intention (insulting versus just pointing out a fact), and you are relying on experience to tell you how to respond.

Now, that is NOT to say that what you're feeling isn't real or valid (it totally is!). Instead, try to remember that your brain is working rapid fire. It's collecting nonstop experiences so that as you grow up, you have a more robust sense of self and other people and be able to respond intuitively to a situation, rather than having to overthink it.

We'll talk about this concept more, because that's kind of the point of this chapter: your brain is learning, adapting, changing, and repeating the process but at a significantly faster rate. So managing your emotions becomes trickier but even more important.

MOODY: AN UNFAIR WORD FOR REAL FEELINGS

Emotions have different intensities. You can feel neutral to having extreme feelings. Maybe the same comment said by a classmate doesn't bug you nearly as much as when your parents say the same thing. Your emotional reaction to a situation can differ by person, place, current stressors, fear, dread—pretty much anything. And they can also build on top of each other, resulting in a bad mood.

When emotions stick around—like someone made you REALLY mad—this is when a fleeting reaction becomes a 'mood.' You've probably heard someone called or yourself been accused of being 'moody' (parents, we're going to have a word about this word...). While I'm not fond of the word, the thought behind it is somewhat valid: teens experience mood swings very quickly and often without warning.

Sense of self (or ego, we sometimes call it) is part of these mood swings: since your brain is preparing you for independent thinking, it can sometimes jump around. Maybe your body needs a little sugar boost (hangry, anyone?) and now that same horrible situation really isn't that bad.

> **FOR THE PARENTS**
>
> Calling your teen moody is name-calling, something we teach our kids *not* to do from a pretty young age... Of course, there should be consequences for misbehavior, but try to remember that your daughter is in the throes of some really extreme mental growth—I like to think of it as mental gymnastics. While I'll give her some tools to try to manage her emotions, give her a break. She's still learning. She's allowed to have emotions. She's allowed to be in a funk from time to time. By calling her moody, you're only driving home the idea that her feelings don't matter, and we both know that you don't believe that.

BENEFITS TO UNDERSTANDING YOUR EMOTIONS

We've talked about understanding your emotions, but we need to talk about the benefits of using this information to help you grow!

EMOTIONS ARE PART OF LIFE

You're going to have emotions, feelings, and reactions every single day for the rest of your life. And it can take a lot of practice to understand the why behind whatever it is that you're experiencing. And as you build life experiences, your 'why' might change, so it helps to start practicing emotional balance as early in life as possible.

It might seem like a lot to take on, what with the influx of feelings you're having thanks to puberty, but now is one of the best times of your life to train your brain.

Sounds weird, but let me explain: because of your increased cognitive development during this phase of life, your brain is more open to learning and retaining information, including how you react. So good habits you form now have a better chance of sticking with you in the long run. This idea applies to exercise, eating, and sleeping, and it also applies to how you end up approaching life.

Consider the benefits by talking through the topics below with your parents.

LIFE CAN BE HARD

I won't sugarcoat it: life has its ups and downs—I hope yours has had mostly ups! But when it comes to handling the tough stuff, it helps to be emotionally prepared (as best you can) so that you can persevere and adapt to whatever situation arises.

This is an example of when it benefits you to know how YOU react to different types of situations, learn from any misinterpretations, and try to handle things differently next time.

→ **PROMPT**: Was there ever a time when you wish you would have responded differently to a confrontation? What happened? Why did you respond as you did? Would you change your reaction now, or would it be the same? Why or why not? (Teens and parents, take turns!)

WHY JUDGE YOURSELF?

When life is hard, or you respond to someone in a way that maybe wasn't how you really wanted to respond, be gentle with yourself.

Now, there's a difference between taking ownership and brushing off your faults, and that's not what we're talking about here. You can still own your mistakes and speak kindly to your inner self.

Just like I reminded your parents a few paragraphs before, you are still learning. And as long as you keep learning and remain open to improving, you shouldn't judge your emotions or your reactions. If you are overly critical of why you are feeling the way you do at any given moment, it doesn't leave much space to actually understand what you're feeling and learn from it.

→ **PROMPT**: Have you ever judged yourself for having certain feelings? How did it feel when you passed judgment? Did it help you resolve your emotional reaction or did it just amplify your feelings? Talk it out and try to find more productive ways to analyze your inner emotions.

PIVOT, PIVOT, PIVOT

Probably one of the trickiest habits to build is learning to pivot. And all I mean is: learn to change your mind, and/or learn to change your approach. (Parents, pay attention to this one!)

We'll talk in more detail about pivoting in the section about self-motivation below. For now, we're talking more about being open to adapting your thinking or approach to yourself and others as you learn.

I'm not saying change your mind every five minutes. I'm saying that all this new information your brain is processing is only as good as you let it be: you have to take how you're feeling, how you choose to react, with how you actually react, and learn from it. Because you suddenly have so much new knowledge and observation skills, you might realize that you will want or need to change your perspective, and sometimes pretty quickly.

STORYTIME

> "I heard someone say once:
> *'It's okay to change your mind.'*
> This simple sentence stuck with me, because I was under the impression that once I said or felt something one time, one way, I was stuck reacting like that each and every time. Now? Now, I let myself react without self-judgment and without worry, even if I'm reacting differently to the exact same situation that I've been in before.
> It's so liberating to just let myself be me."

→ **PROMPT**: It's okay to change your mind! Can you think of two similar situations where you had pretty different reactions? What were the differences? What were the similarities? What do you suppose affected your emotions in each one? Would you change your mind if you found yourself in that same sort of situation once more? Talk it out!

MANAGING YOUR EMOTIONS

Okay, we've talked about your emotions so how might we learn to manage them?

The truth is, you can't always control what you're feeling, but you can try to control how you respond. Here, I'm going to give you a few techniques or tools to help you learn how to manage your emotions, so that you can stay in a more positive headspace and remain open to learning.

✳ TOOL 1: TUNE IN ✳

Spend a day being hyper-aware of your emotions. Be an observer of your own life—what can you learn about your own habits, reactions, feelings? Make some notes, see what you can take into a future encounter that might otherwise seem overwhelming.

✳ TOOL 2: CONNECT WITH YOURSELF ✳

If you know that you're about to have a stressful day (big test, recital, sports game), what can you do to calm yourself beforehand? Do you like bubble baths? Add some lavender. Have excess energy? Put on some calm music and take a stroll. Try to pre-empt your potential negative thoughts with calm ones that remind you that you are in control of the situation.

✳ TOOL 3: BREATHE ✳

Breathing exercises are a tool for a reason—they work! If you find yourself ready to explode at someone or something, take three big breaths. Practice right now. Inhale… exhale… inhale… exhale… inhale… exhale… How are you feeling now?

✳ TOOL 4: FIND AN OUTLET ✳

Sometimes, we cannot control our emotions, and that's okay. But we can find outlets that allow us to be ourselves completely and relax. I kind of think of outlets as happy places—where do you feel the most like you? Is it playing outside? Is it when listening to music laying in the sunshine? Is it coloring? Find your happy place. And whenever you feel like you're starting to spiral, see if you can pull yourself back to a more neutral level at least by engaging in that outlet.

TOOL 5: TIME TO CHAT

For some people, talking through feelings really can help. Maybe you want to talk to your parents, or maybe you want to talk to a friend. Whoever it is, consider trying it to see if you're the kind of person who needs someone just to sit next to you and listen (without offering their thoughts) so that you can work out your emotions.

LET'S PAUSE A MOMENT

How are you feeling?

No, for real, answer the question, because now is a good moment to pause and check in with yourself (and your parents). I totally get it if reading about these different emotions and pressures is making you have a lot of emotions and pressures, because being a teen is stressful.

Before we go further into this topic, it's good to make sure you're in a good headspace and ready to learn. So pause a minute and do the following:

✸ Take a few big breaths

✸ Get up and move your body for a whole minute—dance, stretch, jog in place.

✸ Pour yourself a glass of water

✸ Grab a snack

✸ Need to take a longer break? Jump back in whenever you feel like it's right for you.

Ready? Let's go.

. . .

A RANGE OF EMOTIONS: THANKS A LOT, PUBERTY

We know the why of emotional changes during puberty thanks to the previous section, so now, let's jump into the 'whats.' In other words, what emotions might you experience specifically during puberty and how do these emotions differ from what you used to think of as happy, sad, mad, neutral?

> **FOR THE PARENTS**
>
> Experiencing mood swings, having big, over-the-top emotions—it can be rough, but it's okay. In this next section, we're going to name these emotions to help normalize these changes for your teen. However, keep an eye out for signs that what your teen is going through might be more than just puberty. Have them talk to their doctor or a counselor if needed.
> 1) How long a bad mood lasts: greater than two weeks is a call for concern
> 2) If they seem to go from one extreme to the other very quickly or if they are suddenly much quieter or isolated.
> 3) If they've stopped seeing friends or their grades are dropping significantly.
> 4) Instinct is telling you that something is off or wrong.

YOU MIGHT BE A LITTLE SENSITIVE

Okay, parents, listen up: try to avoid telling your teen that they're being too sensitive—it won't go over well. Not to mention, it's pretty unfair to name-call a very real feeling that's new to them. They are feeling or being sensitive, and that's okay.

So teens, why are you feeling so sensitive? Remember when we talked about being hyper-aware of everything and everyone? Along with that awareness comes some delicate emotions. When you're open learning, you're allowing yourself to be vulnerable, which means that something that used to never bother you, might feel pretty dramatic or upsetting. We'll talk more about trying to manage your emotions, but just know that what you're feeling is very normal.

MISS INDEPENDENT

We talked about independence a few paragraphs above in the context of pushing boundaries. Independence as an emotional state can be a little more complicated. On the one hand, you're very much still a child and you have a heck of a lot to learn about the world. On the other, you are growing up, understanding more each day, and eager to test your wings.

Sometimes, teens impose these ideas of independence on themselves —it's only natural to start thinking more about life after you leave home. Maybe you're developing crushes on other people, or maybe you're dreaming about a career. That craving for adulthood is natural, but you have to be mindful not to let your daydreaming take over your current reality. Yes, work toward goals and allow room for mistakes and fun and being in the present.

And in other cases, parents tend to put unfair pressure on their teens to start acting like adults. It can be arbitrary—you hit a certain age and suddenly your parents think that you should 'know better.' Parents, a gentle reminder that your teens actually don't know much of anything and you pulling out the 'grow up' card doesn't do much good. Amid the chaos of change, your daughter is constantly changing her mind, her outlook on life, even her day to day habits. It's a fine line of teaching your teen responsibility and reminding yourself that she's still got a long road of learning ahead of her.

FINDING YOURSELF IN A CROWD

The turmoil of puberty can almost be simplified into this one thought: you spend these formative years figuring out who you are and who you are going to be.

You probably understand a lot about peer pressure at this point, but let's look at it from another angle. Unfortunately, you won't always have control over how you respond to something happening in your social circle, and that might make you feel a bit icky.

Let's say that you witness a certain behavior and suddenly, you adapt your own behavior to mimic what you saw—maybe someone is getting picked on for their haircut and you join in the prodding, even though you know it's not right.

Did you like what you saw? Maybe not. Did you change your behavior anyway? Yes, you did.

Your social cues—which you are constantly observing, consciously and subconsciously—are also driving your emotions. You don't want to be the one picked on, so you join in to be perceived as part of the group.

Don't put too much blame on yourself if you've done something like this before. Instead, use that icky feeling as a chance to learn what about that interaction you didn't like, so you can train your brain to respond differently in the future.

WHO AM I?

Amid so many emotions and changing moods, you might be feeling a little lost. Stuff that used to interest you a year ago might feel childish now. Or maybe you're not really interested in what your peers are doing and are longing for the days of Legos and monkey bars instead.

It's okay to feel confused, and it's okay to have questions about your identity. And it's absolutely okay to change your mind.

If you're feeling overwhelmed about figuring out who you are, go ahead and check out the exercise at the end of this chapter—bring yourself back to a good mental space.

STORYTIME

> "When I was a kid, I loved Barbie! I loved her outfits, her cars, her accessories. My Barbie was a pilot, a veterinarian, a doctor, a teacher, even a cowgirl! I also really loved HotWheels—I had the parking garages, a whole range of cars, even a racetrack that had like ten loops on it. It was awesome. Then one day, a relative told me that only boys can play with cars and I should stick to dolls. Well, I got so mad at this person that I stopped playing with Barbies, even though I really loved my dolls. I regret that I let that person's opinion matter, because I remember wanting to play with my Barbies but feeling like I had to prove a point."

A DIFFERENT KIND OF SELF REFLECTION

Another common point of confusion when it comes to being yourself? When you look in the mirror, you might not recognize your body. While physical changes don't really happen overnight, it can take your mind some time to realize that your appearance has changed. It's okay if you are nervous about your physical changes or if your body doesn't quite feel like it's yours. These emotions can be amplified when you start to compare yourself to your peers.

IT'S OKAY TO THINK ABOUT SEX

It's not a topic we cover in great detail in this book, because talking about sex is something your parents should take the lead on.

That being said, I want to reassure you that part of puberty is developing sexual maturity—aka, your body's ability to have kids one day. We've talked about menstruation, growing breasts, and even how your body is changing so that childbirth—if you want to have kids one day —is physically easier.

The other part of sexual maturity is thinking about participating in sexual activities. Maybe you got excited by something you saw in a movie, or maybe you're thinking about what it's like to kiss someone —and your body responds physically. What you're feeling is super normal!

You might feel a little bit awkward right this minute, but let me assure you that starting to think about sex is a healthy part of growing up.

In fact, I'd argue that we need to talk a lot more openly about sex, sexual feelings, attraction, and how to be safe if or when you want to act on your feelings. Having sexual thoughts is nothing to be ashamed of and it's important to find a safe adult you can talk to about what you're experiencing.

Parents, talking about sex can feel taboo, probably because our own parents weren't open with us about how normal sexual feelings are. But sexual health and preparedness is a really important topic, and while you might be a little uncomfortable, it's more important to give your daughter a safe space to express whatever it is she needs to share. You don't want her turning to unreliable resources or shaming her for this natural part of life.

A QUICK NOTE

Before we jump into our next topic, a note for the teens and one for the parents. I realized that, in all of this talk about emotions and puberty, we haven't mentioned what happens when other people think they get a say about you, your body, and your feelings.

FOR THE TEENS

I'm a woman so I'm going to be honest: there is always that one jerk who will try to tell you what to do and how to do it. You'll be called bossy, whiny, emotional, sensitive, unladylike. You will be told you aren't girly enough or that you're too girly. You'll get mocked for liking pink and you'll get mocked for hating it. You'll dress too provocatively, or you'll dress too plain. LADIES: ignore them. All of them. Every last one. Use your teens years to figure out who you want to be and know that once you get a little bit older, none of these naysayers will matter at all! You do you, and remember you can change and adapt as much as you want!

FOR THE PARENTS

As we finally enjoy the benefits of modern thinking, it's important to note that the whole 'boys mature slower than girls' belief is a big fat myth. It's unfair to expect girls to exhibit certain behaviors just because they hit puberty and allow boys free range. This kind of attitude is a dangerous stepping stone toward putting absurd social standards on girls: they should be 'nice,' they should be 'patient,' they should be 'put together.' No, girls should be exactly who they are and allowed to have a whole range of emotions and feelings and reactions.

ANXIETY: WHAT IS IT?

The feeling of dread that builds in your stomach, panic tickling your brain, your mind swirling with uncertainty.

Let's name it: Anxiety. It's a bit of a buzzword but that doesn't detract from the power this emotion can have over you.

Some anxiety can be good, a natural although not necessarily ideal sensation that's warning you that something isn't quite right. Sometimes, anxiety is a way for your body to present caution and tell you to pay attention, keep a sharp eye.

Then there are times when anxiety can be too much. It's tricky to always know when your emotions have run away with you, but a good sign is when your worry turns to obsession which then prevents you from acting at all. You can't solve the problem you need to solve because your mind is consumed with the idea of what if instead of what actually is.

That doesn't mean that your anxiety isn't real—it is, because YOU are experiencing it. For example, if going to the doctor and getting a shot makes you anxious, that is 100% real and nothing to be ashamed of. We're only human; we're allowed to have thoughts, emotions, and sometimes irrational reactions to life. What it comes down to, however, is that you learn how to manage your emotions in order to live life on your own terms.

In this section, we're going to talk about all of the points above: how anxiety might manifest itself (positively and negatively), the productive side of a little distress, when and how anxiety might disrupt your life, and how to regain and stay in control.

> **FOR THE PARENTS**
>
> A reminder that what might be making your tween/teen experience anxiety may not be obvious. Whatever it is that's making them anxious, try to understand that their anxiety doesn't have to be rooted in reality. As we'll see in this section, anxious thoughts can spiral out of control quickly. Their worry doesn't have to make sense for it to be real.

> **FOR THE TEENS**
>
> Your parents aren't always going to understand what's stressing you but there are ways you can express yourself so that they can give you the support you need. Read on for some pointers on self-management and to know how to have this tough conversation with the adults in your life.

CAUSES, SIGNS, & WHAT ANXIETY MIGHT LOOK LIKE

CAUSES

A lot of things can cause anxiety. That's not necessarily helpful to hear, but I want to be honest that we can't always control our anxiety. That being said, there are definitely some changes that happen during puberty that might trigger your anxiety.

INDEPENDENCE

It's no secret that, as you get older, you crave independence. It's pretty normal (and healthy!) to want to do things your own way and push back against authority figures who don't give you space to try your hand at making your own choices. The downside to demanding too much independence before you're ready is that you might start to believe that you have to figure everything out on your own. I'll be the first to remind you: you're not alone, although your brain might be telling you otherwise. In this case, your anxiety is taking over, making you feel like no one understands you, that you'll never feel good about yourself, or that you'll always be lonely. But I promise, it does get better.

PEER PRESSURES

You, and everyone around you at school, on teams, in clubs, wherever, feel pressured about growing up. Whether each of you is intending to put this pressure on one another or not, it still exists.

Think about peer pressures like this: your brain (and their brains, too!) is in observation mode pretty much nonstop. This means that you are constantly watching your peers for social cues on how to handle conflict, new information, interactions, and physical comparison. Anxiety can build when you start to project ideas (that aren't based on much of anything) onto these observations.

SOCIAL PRESSURES

Working the same way as peer pressures, social pressure is about the collective group and how different perspectives might get caught up in one way of thinking. For example, there's one teen all the other teens tend to follow, and her leadership changes the dynamic of the entire group. You can feel anxious if you're not in the group or have opinions that might vary from the so-called collective opinion.

SIGNS OF ANXIETY

Anxiety can look different, person by person. There are some common behaviors that people tend to exhibit, but instead of listing those, I am going to give you some real examples to help you understand signs that you might be feeling anxious.

Let's ground the concept of anxiety into something explainable: I like to think of it as WHAT IF.

→ "I really want to try out for the Spring musical, but I'm not sure how I feel about singing in front of dozens of people at the audition."

A normal and relatable statement. We all have things we're scared to try and that can cause dread within us. It's okay and even healthy to be nervous. It's a natural instinct.

→ "I really want to try out for the Spring musical, but I'm sure everyone is going to laugh at me and think I'm a joke."

You want to do something, but you're projecting how others are going to react to you doing it. You have no real basis for your projection, but it's the part you're focused on. The trepidation starts to consume your mind instead of excitement.

→ "I really want to try out for the Spring musical, but I suck at singing and it's not like I'm going to get a part anyway so what's the point?"

In this last scenario, anxiety rears its ugly little head and takes control away from you. We see desire (I want to try out), crippled by doubt (I suck), fueled by unfounded projections (I won't get picked anyway). This statement helps demonstrate the line between "I'm nervous" to debilitating inaction.

Let's dive into a slightly more complicated example.

→ "I have no idea what I'm going to do with my life."

Take it from an adult: every single person the entire world over has had this thought at least once if not dozens of times throughout life. It's important to reflect on what you want to do and who you want to be. Of course, such a question can cause anxiety, but it can be a relatively healthy kind.

→ "I have no idea what I'm going to do with my life and my parents keep pressuring me to make a decision about college."

This anxious thought is complicated but one you're probably familiar with— teens are often stressed about the big 'what's next' and parents about the big 'they aren't taking impending adulthood seriously.'

WHEN ANXIETY STARTS TO TAKE OVER

It's normal to be anxious to some extent—as we've talked about, you are still learning how to read and react to all kinds of new situations.

But sometimes, worry can take over, dominating your thoughts and filling you with doubt.

This is where *choice* and *control* can change your mindset drastically.

Let's use our example from above to work through these concepts:

→ "I have no idea what I'm going to do with my life and my parents keep pressuring me to make a decision about college."

On the one hand, you won't be completely debilitated by inaction: something has to happen after you finish high school, whether you choose that something or it chooses you. But the component of 'pressure' is less tangible, almost like a dark cloud hanging over you. You know you have to make a decision and the pressure from the adults doesn't help.

So you snap and rebel (listen up adults!) and refuse to take ownership of the situation.

Okay teens, your turn to re-read: You refuse to take ownership of the situation.

Whether you like to hear it or not, you're still young and you still have a ton to learn about the world. But at a certain point, you have to start owning your behaviors, actions, and reactions— all of which will ultimately help you maintain control over your emotions, even when they can seem overwhelming.

LET'S PAUSE A MOMENT

These topics might be hitting a little too close to home, perhaps even increasing your anxiety.

We're ready for a short exercise.

✽ Take three deep, full-bellied breaths.

✽ In and out, out and in, holding each breath for a few seconds.

✽ If you didn't complete this little breathing exercise, go back and do it now, before you read any further.

Some of you may refuse to do it anyway (you little rebels, you!) but at least promise to keep this technique in your back pocket: tons of research has been done about the power of taking three deep breaths. It can refocus our minds, calm our pulse, even bring us back from the brink of a panic attack.

Now that you have a simple, use-it-anywhere tool, let's talk about control.

CAN YOU CONTROL THE UNCONTROLLABLE?

What can we actually do to manage our stress or anxiety?

Why do we experience anxiety? Well, because we can't predict the future. More importantly, perhaps, is that we seek control in uncontrollable situations. Anxiety, sneaky emotion that it is, gives us a false sense of control that unfortunately tends to lean toward a negative viewpoint. "I don't know what's going to happen but I'm going to imagine something horrible."

What follows is sweet, sweet relief: that dreadful thing I feared (getting laughed off-stage, failing a test) wasn't actually all that bad (I was cast in a supporting role, I made a B- on the test). You've psyched yourself up so much that it's almost like coming down off of an adrenaline rush.

Maintaining control matters. The highs and lows of anxiety can take a toll on your body, mentally and even physically. If you always fear the worst, panic over the slightest issue, let pressure dictate your life, then control exists outside of your body.

Think about that for a minute: you're not a puppet. You don't want someone telling you how you are supposed to react to a situation—you just want to react! The same is true of anxiety: internal and external pressures are trying to control your worldview. Some of it really is beyond your control (nothing worse than living in limbo) but a lot of it you CAN take responsibility for.

MANAGING ANXIETY IN PRACTICE

Next time a seemingly uncontrollable thought runs your mind, try the following exercise:

Grab some sticky notes and a pen.

→ On a sticky note, write down the impending stressor / project / decision. The "THING" causing you to feel anxious. Example: Apologizing to a friend after a fight.

→ On a different sticky note, write down what you want to happen. How you HOPE it goes. Example: I hope she forgives me, and we can talk about why we ended up fighting, so our friendship is stronger than ever.

→ On the third sticky note, write down your greatest FEAR. Be honest with yourself. Example: She won't forgive me because I screwed up and now I've lost someone I care about. She's going to hate me forever.

→ On the next sticky note, write down the WHAT IF. Example: What if she doesn't forgive me?

→ Finally, on your last sticky note, go ahead and answer the WHAT IF.

Answer that WHAT IF on your own. If your worst fear comes true, then what might actually happen?

Take a long look at the answer you put down. Does it seem a little bit far-fetched? A little bit irrational? Or does it seem okay, like even if the worst happens, whatever happens after that might just be no big deal?

Sometimes in order to control our anxiety, we need to take ownership of it. If you're going to try to project the outcome, then see it through. There is always another step beyond the fear and maybe it really isn't all that bad...

No, you can't always stop your anxiety because you can't always control what happens in life. But you CAN name your fears, sit with your worries, and focus on what you can control.

We'll get more into how to have those tough conversations with yourself (and your parents) in the next section where we'll focus on what negative self-talk is, and how we can reframe our words so that we can reframe our minds.

NEGATIVE SELF-TALK: WHAT, WHY, & REFRAMING

WHAT IS NEGATIVE SELF-TALK

Sometimes, when we're in a bad mood or we're feeling anxious about something, we might hear a little voice inside our minds…

The voice might be overly critical. Maybe it's self-deprecating. Or maybe it's calling you names. Or even worse, it's telling you that you're not good enough.

It's kind of weird, because even though it's our own brain thinking these thoughts, this little voice is almost outside of ourselves.

This is one way of thinking about negative self-talk: bad thoughts we think about ourselves and that we allow to run around in our minds, in turn affecting our emotions and our actions.

WHY DO WE DO NEGATIVE SELF-TALK

Anxiety might play a big role in negative self-talk. But sometimes, negative self-talk is more habit-based than emotional. Even though the words and reactions stem from emotion, sometimes it's helpful to get to the main reason you are talking to yourself unkindly.

CAUSES

Some experts refer to the causes behind negative self-talk more as bad habits. Aka, you aren't dealing with the actual problem and so that little voice inside your head gets in the way of you addressing and resolving a problem.

These bad habits might look like:

- Self-isolation: maybe you need help but you're afraid you'll be judged for it.
- Letting problems linger: the more you stew about a problem the more anxiety you'll have. This can lead to you talking yourself into a corner and letting your negative emotions fester.
- Ignoring your feelings: not taking care of your mental health can lead to you denying what is happening inside your mind. You have to give yourself space to process your emotions, not judge them.
- The company you keep: if you're around people who are speaking unkindly about themselves or you, it can affect how you talk to yourself (and others).

HOW TO STOP NEGATIVE SELF-TALK

In addition to understanding the idea of negative-self talk, you also have to acknowledge (be honest!) if you are participating in it. That's step one. Step two is using some of the following tips to help you start to reframe your thinking:

EVERYTHING IS FIGURE-OUTABLE

Remember that sticky note exercise we did in the section on anxiety? This same exercise can help you put your negative thoughts into perspective, because nothing is ever as bad as it seems.

LIVE IN YOUR FEELINGS

But don't let them get the best of you. Toxic positivity is a real problem, and it's okay to be upset. It's not okay to turn against yourself.

PHONE A FRIEND

Did you mess up? Did you embarrass yourself? Are you starting to spiral into a swirling vortex of panic? Tell someone. Saying what happened out loud, to someone you trust, will take away the power of negative thinking and maybe help you calm down.

REFRAME

Try reframing your words. Instead of, 'I'm so ugly, my face is covered in acne,' try, 'My body is going through a lot, but I'm not the only person going through this.' Reframing doesn't have to be overly positive—in this case, neutral is more realistic because you're still upset by whatever situation you're thinking about negatively, so dismissing those feelings for false happiness doesn't really help you change your mind.

TURNING NEGATIVE SELF-TALK INTO GRATITUDE

Speaking of reframing...

It can be hard to shift your mindset when you feel down or anxious, but it is possible to pull yourself out of a funk and back into a better place.

How do we turn negativity into something positive? Read on!

REFRAMING (AGAIN!)

I can't talk about reframing enough, because it really is how you learn to shift your perspective. A big part of reframing is owning reality but allowing yourself to be thoughtful, positive, or even grateful for a situation. Let's use this example:

→   Negative self-talk: I really screwed up my lines during theater practice today, I'm such an idiot for forgetting what I'm supposed to say.

→   Try: Wow, I messed up my lines today, but thank goodness it was just at rehearsal. I guess I need to practice more.

CHECK YOURSELF

About to spiral and you can already tell it's coming? Stop your thoughts in their tracks. You can do that, trust me. But how?

Give yourself a keyword, or like a safe word for your mind, that says, 'hey, you're about to go down a negative rabbit hole.' Now, maybe you need to dwell a little bit, and that's okay. But once you're done wallowing, use that word and pull yourself out of it.

The idea here isn't to say never have a negative thought, but instead to try to build good habits. That way, whenever something bad or awkward happens, your first instinct isn't to be mad at yourself but instead to separate reality from your projections.

WHAT CAN YOU BE GRATEFUL FOR?

There is something to be said for shifting your mindset completely from negative thinking to positive thinking.

Just because you're a positive person doesn't mean you can't have your bad days—every single person in the world has bad days.

Instead, think of positive thinking as the opposite of negative thinking. In both situations, you're allowed to experience whatever emotions you're having, but the difference is what you do with that experience.

A positive mindset simply means that you try to take the good from a situation, more often than you take the bad. For example, let's say you get a B on a math test. Acknowledging that this grade might be the end of the world for some people and real success for others, let's look at how a negative versus positive thinking might view this experience:

→ NEGATIVE THINKING: A B in math? I'm so stupid, I can't believe I messed up the simple equations.

→ POSITIVE THINKING: A B in math? That sucks. Wow, I really made some mistakes on the simple equations. I better slow down next time so I can get a better grade.

Spot the difference? Positive thinkers think about 'next time.' They acknowledge their disappointment *and* they try to learn from their feelings.

POSITIVE THINKING & GRATITUDE

We've talked a lot about the negative emotions you might experience during your teenage years, but what about the positive ones? If we want to shift our thinking from negative viewpoints and behaviors, then we have to understand positive alternatives.

Positive thinking plays an important role when it comes to gratitude. And gratitude is a very real emotion, one that can come naturally when we're really happy. Other times, gratitude can take work, focus, and practice.

In this last section we're going to look at how to include positive thinking, or gratitude, in little ways throughout your daily life. Gratitude—focusing on the good in your life—is one way to help shift your mindset from negative self-talk and stress into positive energy and long-term happiness.

THE SCIENCE OF GRATITUDE

Have you ever met a person who people refer to as a ray of sunshine?

When we talk about this kind of person, we're not referring to how they look or that they're wearing the color yellow. Instead, we're talking about the energy they exude, almost like they're bringing sunshine to everyone they meet.

Positive energy and gratitude don't have to be big actions—the loudest person in the room is not necessarily the happiest—but they do have to be a part of your daily practice.

Researchers have found some pretty incredible benefits when it comes to spending a little more energy on being grateful, which ultimately leads to a more positive outlook on life:

- Grateful people maintain more control over their lives, able to regulate their emotions with more ease.

- Grateful people have more compassion for others, and are open to understanding different situations and personalities.

- Grateful people tend to be a lot healthier, with less sleep issues, stronger immune systems, and decreased risk of diseases.

- Grateful people learn how to balance their energy and make space for self-awareness and self-care so they have more day-to-day balance.

But why are grateful, positive people enjoying so many benefits? Are their lives somehow easier than ours? No. It's all about perspective and it takes a lot of practice.

So let's try it!

GRATITUDE IN PRACTICE

Here are some simple, easy ways to start shifting your tendency to negative self-talk into positive thinking, all centered around the emotion of feeling grateful.

- Say thank you and mean it! Don't just use the words 'thank you,' but elaborate: thank you for thinking of me when you brought me tulips—they're my favorite flower and I really need a pick-me-up today.

- Be grateful for the small stuff! Like I said, it's easy to be happy in a big moment. But what about when your dad makes you pancakes or waffles (or insert favorite breakfast food here)? That's a sweet gesture, so feel the kindness and let yourself be grateful.

- Make a plan for success! Want to think positively about an upcoming challenge? Write down what you're worried about and where everything can go right. Make sure you're realistic but give yourself space for hope—and make a plan around that.

- Tell your friends that you're grateful for them! Might sound cheesy, but you know what people love? Knowing that we matter to someone else. Think about the last time you helped a friend and they expressed their thanks—it gave you good, warm feelings. Help them feel that way, but without strings attached. Maybe your friend lent you a hair-tie, or maybe she just makes you feel good about life. Tell her that.

- And don't forget about the adults! If your teacher is going above and beyond to help you succeed, acknowledge their help. If your parents got you this book and a new journal for the activities, go ahead and thank them. Sometimes, we don't appreciate adults for all the things they do for us as teens, so say a few kind words.

- Now thank yourself! Look at you—you've made it through some seriously tough topics while reading this book, and I am so proud of you! Show some gratitude toward yourself for having a positive attitude about some pretty complicated topics—you deserve it.

EMOTIONAL CONTROL IN ACTION: EMOTIONAL INTELLIGENCE

In our intro to this chapter, I mentioned that we're going to learn about how to maintain control over our emotional state. This is called **'emotional intelligence'** and the idea is that you can learn to manage your emotions in ways that are both thoughtful and positive, even when you might be feeling anxious or stressed.

When emotions are out of control, your whole brain chemistry changes.

This is a fairly normal part of growing up, so don't feel any kind of way about it.

But contrary to outdated stories, teens do not have to let their emotions completely dominate. And parents don't have to constantly fight with their kids.

It's just a reality that, as a society, we spend a lot of time talking about the challenges of puberty and the teenage years instead of trying to work together to focus on the positives and create a space where we can express ourselves without judgment.

LET'S BE REAL

It can feel like parents and teachers focus a lot on the physical aspects of puberty, but emotional development is a growth spurt by its own rights. As we talked about before, you may suddenly be experiencing amplified feelings. Maybe you feel like all you hear is 'no' or get called moody.

You're not 'moody.' You are just experiencing the world from a totally new perspective, because of those cognitive leaps we've been talking about in this chapter and the previous one.

What does emotional intelligence have to do with the chemical changes that take place during puberty and affect your mood? Well, you can absolutely have your bad days (we all do) but you also have to take ownership of your mental state. That's where EQ can be a game changer. The idea is that if you have high emotional intelligence, then you can better control your mental state despite outsiders' attempts to influence you or disrupt your mood. Emotional intelligence is about awareness and listening to your mental state, including how it might be affecting others.

SPEAKING OF OUTSIDE INFLUENCE

That's the other side of emotional intelligence that we'll focus on: our perception of other people's emotions. For parents and teens alike, EQ also tends to make you more aware and empathetic to other people's emotions. Now, we don't necessarily want to take on those feelings, but we should try to understand different perspectives so that we can learn to read the world around us.

Sometimes, when our bodies are going through change and our hormones are out of whack, we can be a little bit sensitive. A small disagreement might feel like a full-on fight—emotional intelligence helps us to differentiate what raging hormones want us to believe and what's actually going on.

Let's jump into these concepts and build your cognitive capacity so that the emotional rollercoaster of teen-dom doesn't have to be quite so bumpy.

EMPATHY

This component of EQ is about being compassionate. Empathy does not mean that you are supposed to take someone else's emotions and make them your own, but rather that you are able to slow down and try to understand them.

EMPATHY IN PRACTICE

- Listen to listen
- Be aware of your body language
- If you don't want to be called names, then don't name call

> **FOR THE PARENTS**
> Talk to your daughter how you would want her to talk to you, and model for her how you expect others to speak to her— with patience and kindness. Give her examples of empathy in practice by showing her empathy whenever she wakes up grumpy or snaps at you or complains about anything. And make sure you talk about how others should be addressing her, too, so she can learn what is and is not acceptable behavior to give or receive.

SOCIAL SKILLS

As you probably guessed, emotional intelligence has a lot to do with social skills. No, I'm not talking about your ability to be active on five different social media platforms at once. Rather, we're talking about your ability to communicate your ideas and feelings effectively, calmly, and without too much emotional weight attached.

Communication is easier said than done, especially if we're talking about you having to talk to classmates who are going through their own emotional development. But communication doesn't exist in a vacuum—fall back on empathy if you are having trouble expressing yourself or your needs.

SOCIAL SKILLS IN PRACTICE

- Ask others about themselves to build rapport and empathy
- Practice active listening, aka actually listen to the other person's answers
- It's okay to practice social conversations with people you trust—it's hard to know how to handle every situation you're going to encounter socially

SELF AWARENESS

Kind of exactly what it sounds like: you know yourself, your strengths, your weaknesses. You know what might set you off emotionally and where you can step in and be a leader to help others.

But self-awareness in EQ is not just *knowing* how you feel, but *why* you feel that way. You have to take time to build your self-awareness and be prepared to deep dive into your emotions. It's not always the most fun practice, but in the long run, knowing the how and why of your emotional state is a pretty impressive skill!

SELF AWARENESS IN PRACTICE

- Write down your experiences—not just when you're upset, but when you're happy. Focus on the *why* of the emotion.
- Try to figure out what words or concepts trigger you, and, once you have written these down, try to take back the control that these 'triggers' have over you.
- Practice this kind of thinking: your actions don't exist in a bubble, so for every action there's a reaction—so think through what might happen if you take xyz action.

SELF REGULATION

This concept in practice is pretty cool: basically, you're taking your triggering or negative thoughts and turning them into positive, non-triggering ones. You jump from awareness to control.

Self-regulation is especially cool in situations where people expect you to behave a certain way (overreact, shout, lash out) and instead, you remain calm and collected.

It's not just good for personal reasons, though. Self-regulation can be really useful for helping deescalate situations that might otherwise get out of control. For example, maybe two friends are fighting over something and you can help them control their emotions by being the one to express facts or point out that their friendship isn't worth such a silly fight.

SELF-REGULATION IN PRACTICE

- Know that you have emotions and now own them: you control your emotions, not the other way around.
- Keep in mind that you always have a choice when it comes to your reaction—so practice what you might do in different triggering situations.
- Self-regulation also means taking ownership of your emotions. If you know you were mean, apologize. If you know you pushed someone too far, talk to them about why.

SELF MOTIVATION

The final piece of our holistic EQ puzzle is self-motivation. Unlike the previous topics, this one is a little more action-oriented. If you're empathetic, self-aware, able to regulate, and communicate with others, then you can work on self-motivation.

Another way of describing self-motivation might be thinking of this idea as having a growth mindset (a concept we'll really dive into in the next book). For now, think of it like this: you are driven to learn more, do better, be more compassionate, and ultimately, take charge of your life and how you live it.

Phew! That can sound daunting to a teenager (and adults too!), so take a big ol' breath.

SELF MOTIVATION IN PRACTICE

- Have some goals you want to achieve? Write them down! Start with small, realistic goals, so that you can figure out your motivations.
- Then push yourself: want to learn to do a sport or embroider? That's the next level—something still achievable but harder to accomplish without pushing yourself too hard.
- Pivot, pivot, pivot! Something seems impossible? Switch up your approach!

ACTIVITY TIME — GROUNDING TECHNIQUES

We've already worked through a couple of activities in this chapter, but let's add one more to the mix that you can practice as you work on building your emotional intelligence: grounding techniques.

Grounding techniques are helpful with any kind of extreme emotion, although they can be most profound when you're trying to control negative thinking. They can also be useful as a way to calm yourself *before* you start to become overly-emotional.

So what are grounding techniques and how might they help you through the emotions of teen-dom?

WHAT ARE GROUNDING TECHNIQUES

A simple way to understand grounding techniques is to think of them as tools that can help bring the mind away from anxious or over-excited emotions and back into a calmer state of being. And even though we're talking about grounding your emotional state, a lot of grounding techniques use physical distraction or all five senses to help you find your balance.

These seemingly-simple practices will help you root yourself in something real and keep your mind from overthinking or your emotions from spiraling. So let's try a few!

MENTAL GROUNDING TECHNIQUES

Think of mental grounding techniques kind of like playing a game with your mind: you know you're worried about something, but you distract yourself with these practices, instead.

→ Sing your favorite song: it could calm you, but at the very least, trying to recall the words will distract you from whatever is making you spiral.

→ Try an anchoring statement: say a series of real facts that are true right this very minute, like what your favorite color is, recite your address, list off all of your relatives. Anchoring statements remind us that there is reality to our thoughts and make whatever you're stressing about appear that much less real.

→ Describe your surroundings: focus on the smallest details but leave out any opinions. This technique can help you sort through simple facts (the chair is brown) and overthinking (but it has a crack in it and it might break and then...

PHYSICAL GROUNDING TECHNIQUES

Just like the name suggests, physical grounding techniques focus on your body. The idea is to use physical cues to redirect your emotions or thinking.

→ Splash cold water on your face: you'll be surprised how quickly your attention shifts from your problem to feeling the cold. Repeat a few times, taking a deep breath in between splashing.

→ Take a big breath: we tried out a breathing technique before for a good reason—it works. Focus on inhaling and exhaling and nothing else.

→ Stretch: kick off your shoes and lay on the floor. Extend your arms and legs as far as you can and arch your back, stretching your body this way and that, and focus on the physical relief that goes along with it.

5-4-3-2-1 METHOD

Probably one of the most common grounding techniques, the 5-4-3-2-1 approach focuses on all of your senses *and* brings your mind and body back to your immediate present. You don't have to be rigid about how you allocate the numbers—maybe you want to focus on five things you can smell and four things you can see. The idea is to use one sense per number.

So go ahead and give this technique a try, since it's one of the simplest but most effective ways to recenter your mind and body.

→ Five: What are five things you can see? List them, and as you do, notice every detail that you can about whatever it is that you're looking at.

→ Four: Do you smell four different things? Do the smells evoke any kind of emotion?

→ Three: What are three things you can hear? The birds singing? A car horn honking? Let your mind wander as you take in the acoustic cacophony of daily life.

→ Two: What are two things you can touch without moving from wherever you are standing or sitting right this second? The countertop—is it smooth or rough? Cool or warm?

→ One: Is there one thing you can taste? Maybe take a sip of bitter lemonade, or go brush your teeth. Focus on that minty flavor and how the coolness seems to take over your mouth.

WHAT'S NEXT?

Well my friends, we've reached the end of book one of our three part book series!

But this certainly doesn't mean that this is the end for us. Rather, you've only just begun exploring this exciting and somewhat-crazy phase of life. Being a teenager can have its downs, but it can really have its ups, too.

In our next books, we're going to dive deeper into our emotional development and confidence building topics. We'll look at what it means to embrace a growth mindset, and we'll talk about how to build relationships with others while staying true to yourself. We'll also talk safety on the internet and in the real world and much more.

✶ You can get these these next awesome books for free, when you sign up with your email — *see page 3* **✶**

As for this first book, I hope you've found it not just informative, but genuinely helpful!

So before you turn the page and close this little guide, remember two things.

FIRST

You can always come back to the activities and exercises you've learned about here. They are meant to be used many times. Share some of the tools you've learned with your friends. Work together to make these teen years not only fun, but life-changing.

SECOND

You're not alone in any of this. I know it can feel like that. No really, I know firsthand how isolating the teenage years can feel. So look back at the stories, talk to your peers and trusted adults, and never forget that this, too, shall pass.

Until we meet again in the next book!

Feel free to email any questions, thoughts or suggestions to me at:

mazlowepublishing@gmail.com

REFERENCES

Department of Health & Human Services. (n.d.-b). *Puberty*. Better Health Channel. https://www.betterhealth.vic.gov.au/health/healthyliving/puberty

Puberty: Adolescent female - Health Encyclopedia - University of Rochester Medical Center. (n.d.). https://www.urmc.rochester.edu/encyclopedia/content.aspx?contenttypeid=90&contentid=P01635

Puberty Basics (for Teens). (n.d.). https://kidshealth.org/en/teens/puberty.html

Physical changes in puberty. (2024, May 22). Raising Children Network. https://raisingchildren.net.au/pre-teens/development/puberty-sexual-development/physical-changes-in-puberty

Healthdirect Australia. (n.d.). *Puberty for girls*. Physical and Emotional Changes | Healthdirect. https://www.healthdirect.gov.au/puberty-for-girls

Physical development in girls: What to expect during puberty. (n.d.). HealthyChildren.org. https://www.healthychildren.org/English/ages-stages/gradeschool/puberty/Pages/Physical-Development-Girls-What-to-Expect.aspx

Johnson, J. (2024, January 3). *How can I balance my hormones?* https://www.medicalnewstoday.com/articles/324031

Department of Health & Human Services. (n.d.-c). *The menstrual cycle.* Better Health Channel. https://www.betterhealth.vic.gov.au/health/conditionsandtreatments/menstrual-cycle#phases-of-the-menstrual-cycle

Period products: What teens need to know. (n.d.). https://www.nationwidechildrens.org/family-resources-education/700childrens/2021/05/period-products-teens

Puberty 101: The Clue guide to getting your period (Part 1) (2021, February 15). https://helloclue.com/articles/life-stages/puberty-101-clue-guide-to-getting-your-period-part-1

NHS inform. (2023, May 4). *Periods (menstruation) | NHS inform.* NHS Inform. https://www.nhsinform.scot/healthy-living/womens-health/girls-and-young-women-puberty-to-around-25/periods-and-menstrual-health/periods-menstruation

Menarche. (2024, May 1). Cleveland Clinic. https://my.clevelandclinic.org/health/diseases/24139-menarche

Nm, W. S. O. (2020, July 29). *Puberty and your Menstration Cycle - WSNM.* WOMENS SPECIALISTS OF NEW MEXICO. https://wsnm.org/education/teen-healthcare-albuquerque/puberty-and-your-menstration-cycle/

The growing child: adolescent 13 to 18 years. (2024, August 29). Johns Hopkins Medicine. https://www.hopkinsmedicine.org/health/wellness-and-prevention/the-growing-child-adolescent-13-to-18-years

All about periods (for teens). (n.d.). https://kidshealth.org/en/teens/menstruation.html

Menstruation in girls and Adolescents: Using the menstrual cycle as a vital sign. (n.d.). ACOG. https://www.acog.org/clinical/clinical-guidance/committee-opinion/articles/2015/12/menstruation-in-girls-and-adolescents-using-the-menstrual-cycle-as-a-vital-sign

Ruby Cup. (2019, May 2). *How much do you bleed on your period? What research says.* https://rubycup.com/blogs/articles/how-much-do-you-bleed-on-your-period

Physical development in teens. (n.d.). UMN Extension. https://extension.umn.edu/teen-development/biological-and-physical-changes-teens

Campbell, J. (2024, March 11). Menstrual cycle snacking: Why you crave chocolate during your period. *Women's Health Australia.* https://www.womenshealth.com.au/an-expert-explains-why-you-crave-chocolate-during-your-period/

Body image: pre-teens and teenagers. (2022, September 12). Raising Children Network. https://raisingchildren.net.au/pre-teens/healthy-lifestyle/body-image/body-image-teens#:~:text=Your%20child%27s%20body%20image%20is,is%20-going%20through%20many%20changes

McShirley, C. (2015, August 21). What is Body Image? PsychAlive. https://www.psychalive.org/what-is-body-image/

Body image | Office on Women's Health. (n.d.). OASH | Office on Women's Health. https://www.womenshealth.gov/mental-health/body-image-and-mental-health/body-image

Department of Health & Human Services. (n.d.-a). *Body image - women.* Better Health Channel. https://www.betterhealth.vic.gov.au/health/healthyliving/body-image-women

Mayer, B. A. (2024, September 9). *What is an 'Almond mom'? and why Being one can be harmful.* Parents. https://www.parents.com/what-is-an-almond-mom-and-how-to-not-be-one-6822156

Why exercise is wise (for teens). (n.d.). https://kidshealth.org/en/teens/exercise-wise.html

Physical activity: pre-teens and teenagers. (2023, February 23). Raising Children Network. https://raisingchildren.net.au/teens/healthy-lifestyle/physical-activity/physical-activity-teens

The Importance of Physical Fitness for Teens. (n.d.). Littletikescommercial.

https://littletikescommercial.com/blog/physical-fitness-teens/?lang=can

Physical Activity Facts | Healthy Schools | CDC. (n.d.). https://www.cdc.gov/healthyschools/physicalactivity/facts.htm#:~:text=Regular%20physical%20activity%20can%20help,developing%20health%20conditions%20such%20as%3A&text=Heart%20disease.,Type%202%20diabetes

Create a life balance wheel - E-Classroom. (n.d.). https://e-classroom.co.za/blog/create-a-life-balance-wheel

SamaritanFamilyWellness.org. (n.d.). Teen Wellness Self-Assessment. In *SamaritanFamilyWellness.org* (pp. 1–5). https://static1.squarespace.com/static/5b54fe275ffd2051be834f8c/t/5c5c9e8c9140b77d1c907638/1549573784643/Teen+Self+Assessment.pdf

BSEd, P. M., & BSEd, P. M. (2019, July 23). *5 Activities to Help Moms Bond with Their Teen Daughters.* Child Development Institute. https://childdevelopmentinfo.com/child-activities/5-activities-help-moms-bond-teen-daughters/

5-4-3-2-1 coping technique for anxiety. (n.d.). https://www.urmc.rochester.edu/behavioral-health-partners/bhp-blog/april-2018/5-4-3-2-1-coping-technique-for-anxiety.aspx

Aid, T. (2020, September 22). *Grounding techniques.* Therapist Aid. https://www.therapistaid.com/therapy-article/grounding-techniques-article

Raypole, C. (2024, January 29). *30 Grounding techniques to quiet distressing thoughts.* Healthline. https://www.healthline.com/health/grounding-techniques#physical-techniques

Living Well. (2019, September 13). *Grounding exercises - Living Well.* Living Well - a Resource for Men Who Have Been Sexually Abused or Sexually Assaulted, for Partners, Family and Friends and for Professionals. https://livingwell.org.au/well-being/mental-health/grounding-exercises/

The science behind gratitude (and how it can change your life). (n.d.). happify.com. https://www.happify.com/hd/the-science-behind-gratitude/

Hilton Andersen, C. (2024, March 11). *7 Simple Ways to Practice Gratitude in Your Everyday Life*. Reader's Digest. https://www.rd.com/article/how-to-practice-gratitude/

Galindo, P. C. Y. M. (2024, August 5). What is gratitude? 12 tips for how to start a gratitude practice. *BetterUp*. https://www.betterup.com/blog/gratitude-definition-how-to-practice

Reid, S. (2024, August 29). Gratitude: the benefits and how to practice it. *HelpGuide.org*. https://www.helpguide.org/articles/mental-health/gratitude.htm

Conlon, C. (2023, March 24). *40 simple ways to practice gratitude*. LifeHack. https://www.lifehack.org/articles/communication/40-simple-ways-practice-gratitude.html

Staff, M. (2024, October 27). *How to practice gratitude*. Mindful. https://www.mindful.org/an-introduction-to-mindful-gratitude/

3 Ways to practice gratitude (for teens). (n.d.). https://kidshealth.org/en/teens/gratitude-practice.html

Cafasso, J. (2023, September 28). *Tips to Help You Mentally and Emotionally Cope with Metastatic Breast Cancer*. Healthline. https://www.healthline.com/health/rethink-bc-negative-self-talk#Address:-Stop-it-in-its-tracks

How to Stop Negative Self-Talk - Headspace. (n.d.). Headspace. https://www.headspace.com/mindfulness/stop-negative-self-talk

Wilson, T., Timmerman, P., Salvatore, S., Hrychuk, A., & Pushkareva, D. (2021b, May 6). *Learn to use positive self-talk for a successful career in 6 min*. Rumie-learn. https://learn.rumie.org/jR/bytes/learn-to-use-positive-self-talk-for-a-successful-career-in-6-min/?gclid=CjwKCAjwitShBhA6EiwAq3RqAztNKH3xvq-kdUShctIGv1KfsF0XmWBs3QjcD2LGf8HoOKzdf0MfDhoCzMgQAvD_BwE

Ms, E. Q. (2021, July 4). *How imagery and visualization can improve athletic performance*. Verywell Fit. https://www.verywellfit.com/negative-self-talk-6501077

Amymin. (2021, February 10). *The Origin of Your Negative Self-Talk - Amy Eliza Wong*. Amy Eliza Wong. https://www.alwaysonpurpose.com/2014/10/the-origin-of-your-negative-self-talk/

B, O. (n.d.). *Causes of negative self talk and how to overcome it*. https://www.olympiabenefits.com/blog/causes-of-negative-self-talk-and-how-to-overcome-it#:~:text=What%20Causes%20Negative%20-Self%2DTalk,are%20causing%20negative%20self%2Dtalk

City, M. C. a. T. I. N. Y. (2023, June 9). *The Ultimate Guide to Understanding Your Feelings & Emotions for 2022*. Mindwell NYC. https://mindwellnyc.com/the-ultimate-guide-to-understanding-your-feelings-emotions-for-2022/

Understanding your emotions (for teens). (n.d.). https://kidshealth.org/en/teens/understand-emotions.html

Sutton, J. (2020, October 7). *Understanding Emotions: 15 Ways to Identify Your Feelings*. PositivePsychology. https://positivepsychology.com/understanding-emotions/

5 Ways to Know your Feelings Better (for Teens). (n.d.). https://kidshealth.org/en/teens/emotional-awareness.html

David, S. (2017, September 21). *3 Ways to Better understand your emotions*. Harvard Business Review. https://hbr.org/2016/11/3-ways-to-better-understand-your-emotions

Healthdirect Australia. (n.d.-a). *Helping your child through puberty*. Healthdirect. https://www.healthdirect.gov.au/emotional-changes-puberty

Emotional changes that occur during puberty. (n.d.). https://www.menstrupedia.com/articles/girls/emotional-changes

Mood swings and puberty. (2023, October 11). Kids Helpline. https://kidshelpline.com.au/parents/issues/mood-swings-and-puberty#:~:text=They're%20creating%20changes%20on,feel%20intense%20and%20complex%20emotions

Team, C. (2024, March 14). *15 Powerful benefits of Emotional Intelligence Training.* Continu. https://www.continu.com/blog/15-benefits-of-emotional-intelligence-training

Lpc, S. S. (2022, March 18). *The Importance of Managing Emotions: Modern therapy.* Modern Therapy. https://moderntherapy.online/blog-2/2020/5/9/the-importance-of-managing-emotions

Understanding your emotions (for teens). (n.d.-b). https://kidshealth.org/en/teens/understand-emotions.html#:~:text=Emotional%20awareness%20helps%20us%20know,past%20difficult%20feelings%20more%20easily

What is emotional intelligence, Daniel Goleman. (2023, September 7). Last Eight Percent. https://www.ihhp.com/meaning-of-emotional-intelligence/

What is emotional intelligence and how does it apply to the workplace? (n.d.). Mental Health America. https://mhanational.org/what-emotional-intelligence-and-how-does-it-apply-workplace

MSEd, K. C. (2024, January 31). *You Can Increase Your Emotional Intelligence in 3 Simple Steps—Here's How.* Verywell Mind. https://www.verywellmind.com/what-is-emotional-intelligence-2795423

EWF International. (2022b, September 14). *5 components of emotional intelligence You need to become a more effective leader.* https://ewfinternational.com/5-components-emotional-intelligence-effective-leadership/#:~:text=Goleman%27s%20EQ%20theory%20comprises%20five,skills%20that%20make%20up%20EQ

www.ingramcontent.com/pod-product-compliance
Lightning Source LLC
Chambersburg PA
CBHW052148070526
44585CB00017B/2025